My Life's Soul~Journey

Daily Meditations
For Ever-Increasing Spiritual Fulfilment

Sri Chinmoy

AUM
PUBLICATIONS

Compiled by Paripurnata.
Copyright © 1995 Sri Chinmoy

ISBN: 0-88497-244-5
Printed by:
Aum Publications
86-10 Parsons Blvd.
Jamaica, NY 11432

INTRODUCTION

Whether we are new to the spiritual life or advanced seekers, we all welcome daily opportunities for self-transformation—opportunities to overcome anger, develop more confidence, become more self-giving, listen to our inner voice and surrender to God's Will.

This collection of Sri Chinmoy's aphorisms, poems and reflections is designed to inspire God-lovers of all levels as they walk along the road to self-perfection. Penned by a realised spiritual Master, these writings provide nuggets of truth and wisdom that will allow us to hold fast to higher ideals throughout each day.

—Paripurnata

BEGINNING

FROM THE SPIRITUAL POINT OF VIEW, EVERY seeker is a beginner. A beginner is he who has the inner urge to grow into something ever more divine, ever more illumining and ever more fulfilling. The moment you want to make constant and continuous progress, the moment you want to constantly surpass yourself and enter into the ever-transcending Beyond, at that moment you become an eternal beginner.

If you are an absolute beginner, then you have to start by reading a few spiritual books or scriptures. These will give you inspiration. It is also a good idea to associate with people who have been meditating for some time. These people are not in a position to teach you; far from it. But they will be able to inspire you.

In the beginning you should not even think about meditation. Just try to set aside a certain time of day when you will try to be calm and quiet, and feel that these five minutes belong to your inner being and to nobody else. Regularity is of paramount importance. What you need is regular practice at a regular time.

For a beginner it is better to start with concentration. Otherwise, the moment you try to make your mind calm and vacant, millions of uncomely thoughts will enter into you and you will not be able to meditate even for one second. But if you concentrate, at that time you challenge the wrong thoughts that are entering you. So in the beginning, just practise concentration for a few minutes. Then, after a few weeks or a few months, you can try meditation.

When you start meditating, try always to feel that you are a child. When one is a child, one's mind is not developed. At the age of twelve or thirteen, the mind starts functioning on an intellectual level. But before that, a child is all heart. A child feels that he does not know anything. He does not have any preconceived ideas about meditation and the spiritual life. He wants to learn everything fresh from the mother and father.

First feel that you are a child, and then try to feel that you are standing in a flower garden. This flower garden is your heart. A child can play in a garden for hours. He goes from this flower to that flower, but he does not leave the garden, because he gets joy from the beauty and fragrance of each flower. Feel that inside you is a garden, and you can stay in it for as long as you want. In this way you can learn to meditate in the heart.

If you can remain in the heart, you will begin to feel an inner cry. This inner cry, which is aspiration, is the secret of meditation. When a grown-up person cries, his cry is usually not sincere. But when a child cries, even if he is crying only for candy, he is very sincere. At that time, candy is the whole world for him. If you give him a hundred-dollar bill, he will not be satisfied; he cares only for candy. When a child cries, immediately his father or mother comes to help him. If you can cry from deep within for peace, light and truth, and if this is the only thing that will satisfy you, then God, your eternal Father and eternal Mother, is bound to come and help you.

You should always try to feel that you are as helpless as a child. As soon as you feel that you are helpless, somebody will come to help you. If a child is lost in the street and he begins to cry, some kind-hearted person will show him where his home is. Feel that you are lost in the street and that there is a storm raging outside. Doubt, fear, anxiety, worry, insecurity and other undivine forces are pouring down on you. But if you cry sincerely, somebody will come to rescue you and show you how to get to your home, which is your heart. And who is that somebody? It is God, your Inner Pilot.

Each person's soul has its own way of meditating. My way of meditating will not suit you, and your way of meditating will not suit me. There are many seekers whose meditation is not fruitful because they are not doing the meditation that is right for them. If you do not have a spiritual Master who can guide you, then you have to go deep within and get your meditation from the inmost recesses of your heart.

Today you may be a beginner in the spiritual life, but do not feel that you will always be a beginner. At one time everybody was a beginner. If you practise concentration and meditation regularly, if you are really sincere in your spiritual search, then you are bound to make progress. The important thing is not to be discouraged. God-realisation does not come overnight. If you meditate regularly and devotedly, if you can cry for God like a child cries for his mother, then you will not have to run to the Goal. No, the Goal will come and stand right in front of you and claim you as its own, very own.

JANUARY

Only when you listen
To the dictates of your soul,
The path ahead of you
Becomes absolutely clear.

There are two mighty forces that govern this world of ours. These mighty forces are desire-night and aspiration-light.

Desire-night is the love of power, and aspiration-light is the power of love. The love of power wants to destroy and devour the entire world. The power of love wants to feed and immortalise the entire world. The love of power is self-love; the power of love is God-love. When we utilise the love of power in our day-to-day activities, we consciously and deliberately bring to the fore the destructive vital anger in us. When we utilise the power of love in our multifarious activities, then God, out of His infinite Bounty, showers His choicest Blessings on us.

Keep your heart open
To the power of love
If you want to be
In close contact with God.

Life has an inner door. Aspiration opens it. Desire closes it. Aspiration opens the door from within. Desire closes it from without.

If we aspire to become great, then our aspiration is not real aspiration. If we aspire to become good, then our aspiration is real, divine aspiration. Goodness is the aim of true aspiration. Greatness is constant competition. There is no satisfaction in it. By competition alone we can never achieve satisfaction. But if we become good, if we become divine instruments of God, then we achieve satisfaction far beyond our imagination's flight.

You can dream of the horizon.
You can build a new world.
But do not forget,
The heart of Mother-Earth
Gave you the inspiration-light
And aspiration-delight.

If we walk along the road of desire-night, fulfilment will always remain a far cry.

Yesterday we had one house; today we want two houses. If we get two houses today, we will not be satisfied. Tomorrow we will want to have one more. No matter how many things we possess, we will not be satisfied. Each time our expectation is fulfilled, a new expectation will come to take its place. But if we live in aspiration-light, when we achieve even an iota of satisfaction, we feel that inside that satisfaction one day will loom large infinite, boundless satisfaction. The aspiration-road must be followed. Each individual seeker must live in aspiration-light if he wants satisfaction. If he lives in desire-night, there can never be satisfaction.

Because of your desire-life,
God comes and goes in your heart.
He will take up permanent residence
Inside your heart
Only when you become
Your life's climbing aspiration-cry.

Self-giving alone has a free access to joy everlasting.

Each individual on earth is crying for only one thing and that is satisfaction. But if satisfaction comes, it has to come through self-giving. Self-giving is the precursor of God-becoming. The more consciously and soulfully we can give our body, vital, mind, heart and soul to the Supreme Pilot within us, the sooner we can become an exact prototype of His divine existence.

Happiness in cheerful self-giving
Is beyond compare.
It is the highest delight
That God has created for humanity.

When we nurture our weaknesses, we shake hands with the breath of painful compromise.

How do you cure meanness? Not by thinking of meanness all the time. From now on, kindly take the positive side. Meanness is self-centred. By always thinking of night, by always looking at night, you cannot go into light; whereas if you consciously think of vastness, the sympathetic heart or oneness-heart, then automatically meanness disappears from you.

Train your mind to obey you.
Train your life
To surrender to your heart.
Happiness will be your permanent property.

Each seeker has two individuals in him: one is the desiring man, the other is the aspiring man.

The world has offered you considerable frustration. Who is responsible for this frustration? The desiring man in you. The aspiring man in you will never be frustrated; he will always try to see light in God's own way. If constantly you feel the presence of the desiring man, he will give you what he has: frustration. Then you will see no purpose in life. But if you feel the aspiring man in yourself, then at every moment you will see a glowing purpose in your life. Each thought, each idea, each ideal will have a purpose. Each moment will have a purpose. Inside each moment you will see a vast, conscious operation. So if you want to discover the purpose of your life, from now on kindly try to feed and nourish the aspiring man in you. Then you are bound to discover the purpose in your life.

You are not your mind's
Desire-jungle.
You are not your vital's
Destruction-beast.
You are your heart's
Aspiration-lamp.

Today's problems are killing you. Why do you want to be totally annihilated by inviting tomorrow's problems?

All past, present and future problems put together are helpless in the face of aspiration, for aspiration is the burning, glowing flame within. It is a birthless and endless flame that mounts high, higher, highest and purifies the things that have to be purified in our unlit, obscure, impure nature. While illumining the unlit, obscure, impure qualities in us, it immortalises the divine qualities in us: faith in God, love of God and unconditional surrender, which says to God, "Let Thy Will be done."

All your vital problems
Will vanish
And you will be able to weather
All your inner storms
When you develop sleepless aspiration
And when dedication
Becomes your second nature.

Love is a bird. When we encage it, we call it human love. When we allow love to fly in the all-pervading Consciousness, we call it divine love.

If we give someone something and then expect something in return because we feel that the person is under an obligation to give us something back, this is human love. But if we can do something unconditionally, that is divine love. In divine love we give for the sake of giving and we feel it is up to the other person whether he gives us something back or not. This is unconditional love; this is divine love.

Every time you love unconditionally,
A winged angel flies down
And tells you,
"Sit down on my wing quickly!
The Lord Supreme is waiting for you."

Talk and act always from the heart of your generosity.

When you really have something to offer to the world, then you can become truly humble. A tree, when it has no fruit to offer, remains erect. But when the tree is laden with fruit, it bends down. When you have genuine humility, it is a sign that you have something to offer to mankind. If you are all pride and ego, then nobody will be able to get anything worthwhile from you.

Pray that God
Will not only use your willingness,
But also transform your haughtiness
Into selflessness.

Your heart must learn how to renew soul-fully every day the splendour of your inner wealth.

To enter the spiritual life, you have to feel the necessity of the inner life. You have to feel that if you are secure and satisfied in the inner world, only then will you have security and satisfaction in the outer world. The spiritual life will give you inner peace, joy and bliss in abundant measure. People cry for name, fame, earthly achievement, success and progress and so many things. They are right in their own way. But if you want to enter the spiritual life, you should start crying inwardly from this moment on for joy, peace of mind and the awakening of your inner consciousness.

If you are ready
To close your mind
When it is needed,
If you are ready
To expose your vital
When it is needed,
Then God will be all ready
To receive your heart
When it is needed.

Ego-gratification is always an unprofitable business.

Your very nature, your very soul, your very existence wants to remain in the Infinitude. If one remains in the highest light, in the all-fulfilling light, then it is for the light to decide whether the light wants to give a specific experience to an individual seeker by giving him name and fame and so forth. But if the seeker wants to have both desire and aspiration together, both worldly name and fame and true aspiration for the Highest, then he will be neither in the spiritual life nor in the ordinary, material life because constantly he will be pulled by two contradictory forces.

There was a time
When I wanted name and fame.
That was my human desire.
But now
I want only to manifest God
In His own way.
Indeed, this is my divine aspiration.

When we pay all attention to the material world and neglect the inner world, we starve the soul in us. The soul has to be brought to the fore. If we think that we can get infinite wealth from the material world, then we are totally mistaken.

There is a difference between spiritual wealth and material wealth. When you use money properly, you can enjoy it for some time, but gradually it disappears. But if you use spiritual wealth, which is peace, light and bliss, properly, if you give it to the right person, then automatically the Supreme fills your receptacle, the vessel inside your heart. If you start with an iota of peace and you use it in a divine way, then the Supreme is bound to give you abundant peace. If you start using the qualities of peace, light and bliss properly, in a divine way, then when you are disturbed or agitated by the wrong forces of the outer world, I assure you that the Source will supply you with more peace, light, bliss and all other divine qualities.

It is not inevitable
That some people become rich
While others remain poor.
No, it entirely depends on
Their eagerness for wealth.
Even so, your spiritual wealth
Depends on your eagerness
To become spiritually wealthy.

To fulfil his divine destiny, man has to be conscious of his inner reality and his soul's oneness with the Supreme.

An ordinary, unaspiring heart is bound to suffer from insecurity and a sense of separativity. That heart will not dare to unify itself with other hearts, for it thinks that it will lose everything that it already has. But the transformed spiritual heart feels that the more it identifies itself with other hearts, the sooner it will get peace, light and bliss in abundant measure. A transformed heart is the heart that has established its inseparable and eternal oneness with all and sundry. It feels that the moment it becomes vast, it will have satisfaction and it will be able to claim the entire creation as its very own. Instead of losing, it feels that it will gain everything: the entire creation plus the Creator Himself.

Why are you so anxious
To be left alone?
If you want satisfaction
From your life,
Then there is only one way
To achieve it,
And that is by establishing
Your sleepless oneness
With the world.
There is no other way!

The inner teaching teaches us how to love mankind and how to serve the divinity in humanity.

How can we acquire the true love for humanity? In order to love humanity, we have to go to the Source. The Source is not humanity; the Source is Divinity. If we really can go to the Source and love Divinity, then we see that Divinity is not something apart from our real existence. First we have to love God, who is Divinity itself. If we can love God, then we will feel that our inner existence cannot be separated from God. Our true divine existence and God are one. Then we will see what our outer existence is. Our outer existence, which is divine personality, is the entire humanity. Humanity is not around you or outside you; it is inside you. If you become one with your divine existence, then you will see that inside you is the entire humanity. Whatever is inside you is yours; whatever is outside you is not yours. You can help to fulfil and illumine only that which is inside. So you have to feel that humanity is inside you. Then you will be able to love and serve humanity truly and effectively.

To solve every problem,
Solve your own problems first.
To love each and every human being,
Love God first.

To touch the world-heart, give your life to God's all-seeing Will.

If we feel God's presence in each action, then automatically it becomes wisdom because God is all wisdom. Before we say anything, we need approval. Our direction we must get from within. God will not remain silent; He will not be indifferent. God appears to remain silent only because we do not go deep within in order to hear His Voice, His Dictates. He is not like an indifferent human being whom we ask again and again without getting any answer. Go deep within. Immediately God will answer either yes or no.

There are two steps
To self-transformation:
I do not know,
And
I know because
My Beloved Supreme teaches me
How to know, what to know
And why to know.

Allow not your mind to act freely, for it may either lead or follow evil thoughts.

The best thing is not to use the mind to execute anything unless and until you have heard from the inner Source what you should do or what you should say. If you are prompted to do something, but you have not gone deep within, do not do it. Before we actually execute what we feel like doing, let us go deep within. When it is an important matter, the best thing is not to even think of doing anything without going deep within. That is wisdom.

My mind does not know
Where it is going.
My heart does not know
Why it is crying.
My life does not know
Why it is failing.
But I do know
What I am doing:
I am doing what I am inspired to do
From within.

God knows what is best for you. Make this a psychic realisation and not just a mental conviction.

When we pray, we feel that God will listen to our prayer. When we meditate, we feel that we will receive peace, light and bliss, which is an absolutely true and legitimate claim. But when we pray, when we meditate, we have to feel that it is our business to pray and meditate and it is God's business either to give us peace or not to give us anything. We have to come to that kind of surrender. We shall play our part by praying and meditating; that is our task. God's task is to feed us with His Light, Peace and Bliss. But He knows the right moment. So if we can meditate, and during our meditation if we have the feeling that we shall not expect anything—that if peace, light and bliss enter into us, well and good; if not, then we will be equally satisfied—then this will be the best type of meditation. We shall meditate because we feel that it is the only way we can become inseparably one with God.

If you really love God
And need only God,
Then give God the opportunity
To care for you
Always in His own way.

When we become really humble, we offer more of our capacity, divinity and reality. Only by becoming humble can we become what we truly are. We become of greater use, of greater help to mankind.

Humility we have to take as a divine gift and a supreme gift. It is something that we have to offer to mankind. We have to feel that humility is our feeling of consecrated oneness with humanity. If we take humility in the highest and purest sense of the term, then we can become really humble. Humility is not a matter of touching the feet of somebody, no. It is something that has to be shared with the rest of the world. It is the God-life within us. The higher we go, the greater is our promise to the Supreme in mankind. The more light we receive by virtue of our humility, the more we have to offer to mankind.

Every day
You must practise humility
And fold your proud hands
In Heaven-climbing prayers.

Where your sacrifice is, there will as well be your delight.

There are two types of sacrifice: earthly sacrifice and Heavenly sacrifice, material sacrifice and spiritual sacrifice. Material sacrifice we all know very well: we give money, or we give material objects to others. But spiritual sacrifice is something else. In spiritual sacrifice we give peace, bliss, inner power and other divine qualities. Undoubtedly, spiritual sacrifice is far more important than material sacrifice. Material sacrifice does not demand much concentration. If you do not like something you have, such as a piece of furniture, then you can give it away. But if you want to offer peace to somebody else, then you have to pray and meditate for a long, long time so that you can acquire this peace within you.

How can one get the greatest joy?
Not by possessing, but by sacrificing.

Use your heart and you will see God in all human beings.

We cannot separate God from our existence or from our imperfections. Do you think that God is not there in all the imperfections that we see in this world? God is everywhere, but He is manifested to different degrees. God is in the thief as well as in the honest person. He is there, having an experience. God is in everything. He is in the highest and He is also in the lowest.

Today
I am determined
To give space
To the unloved ones.

What is meant by spiritual perfection? It is the constant capacity to live in God and to reveal Him in one's every movement.

The only way you can show the existence of God to a person who does not believe that God exists is by your own personal inner peace, inner light and inner joy. You can show the Supreme in any of the infinite aspects or infinite ways in which He manifests Himself. Since the Supreme is infinite joy, peace, light, bliss and power, you can reveal Him just by embodying these qualities in yourself. Your very appearance, your very presence, when you stand in front of that person, can make him feel the existence of God inside you.

To see
A face of love
Is to feel
A heart of peace.

Each day you pray and meditate soulfully, you are bound to spread your heart's oneness-fragrance powerfully.

The best way to convince someone of the existence of God is to try to manifest His Divinity in your own life. If the other person is at all sincere or receptive, he will see that you have something that he lacks. He will also feel that your qualities of light and peace are coming from another source. He knows that you are leading a spiritual life. He knows that you believe in God. He will see and feel that you have got inner peace, poise, light and joy. If he is sincere, that is all the proof he needs. His inner perception of a better, higher consciousness in you is the only thing that will convince him. It will convince him more than thousands of words.

Each soul is God's
Direct representative on earth.
Therefore
It is authorised to exercise
Its God-ordained dignity.

What is it, after all, that gives to a child his charm and beauty? Is it not the soul's glow? When that touch gets fainter and is finally lost, he becomes a dull and cautious adult.

Always try to feel that you are God's child. Early in the morning you can soulfully repeat, "I am God's child, I am God's child, I am God's child." Immediately you will see that whatever is dark, impure and ugly in you will go away. Later in the day, when ignorance comes to tempt you, you will feel, "I am God's child. How can I do this? I cannot enter into ignorance." By repeating, "I am God's child," you will get abundant inner strength and will-power.

My Lord Supreme,
How can I avoid
Disobeying You unconsciously?
"My child,
If you have constant eagerness
To please Me in My own way,
Then automatically
Unconscious disobedience
Will disappear."

If you devote yourself to something or to someone, then sooner or later you will achieve success in whatever you aspire for.

You have to constantly ask yourself one thing: do you want God or do you want ignorance? Both are standing right in front of you at every moment, and you must make a choice. One cannot serve two masters. When these two masters stand in front of you, you have to decide immediately which one you want. If you choose God, then you must come to Him and enter into Him. And each time you find that you have come out of a divine consciousness, you have to enter into it again. If you can re-enter into God's Consciousness faithfully every time you come out of it, then eventually you will reach the point where you will not come out of it and enter into ignorance anymore. A day will come when your conscious choice of God will be permanent and you will be totally merged in God forever.

Do not think
That you cannot do it.
Just think that God
Is definitely going to do it
In you, for you.

An ordinary person needs hope in order to make any move forward, and if there is no forward movement, then self-destruction starts. Without hope, life for an ordinary person becomes a stagnant pool. But if you have sincere aspiration, you do not have to worry; you will get everything.

How can we avoid losing hope? We must try to cast aside all expectations from our desiring mind. It is our outer mind which feels that it needs something or wants something. When we feel that we need something, hope begins to play its part. It is the desiring mind that feeds our outer hope. If we can be above the desiring mind and remain all the time in the spontaneity of the heart, then we will have a constant feeling of possessing the divine truth. Our inner heart is always full and complete, requiring nothing. When we need nothing, hope does not enter into the picture, for it is not at all necessary. When you remain with your heart's aspiration, you are constantly identified with God's Will, and at that time your earthly hope is transformed into divine hope.

Hope is sweet.
Hope is illumining.
Hope is fulfilling.
Hope can be everlasting.
Therefore, do not give up hope,
Even in the sunset of your life.

It does not matter if the result is success or failure. If we are not at all attached to the results, we get an immediate expansion of consciousness. If we do not care for the fruit of our action, the Supreme rewards us in the Supreme's own way.

God Himself is above both success and failure. If you want to become identified totally and inseparably with God's Will, then think of neither success nor failure. Think only of pleasing the Supreme. According to our human eyes the fulfilment of hope is success. But the fulfilment of God's Will goes far beyond so-called failure or success, and this is what is of paramount importance. Divine fulfilment is always beyond outer results. We understand the results and we derive the utmost benefit from the results only when we are unreservedly one with God's Will.

A seeker's heart
Cares for neither success
Nor failure.
A seeker's heart
Longs for the seeker's
Constant acceptance of God
And
God's constant,
Unconditional experience
In and through the seeker's life.

Surrender begins not in helplessness but in the acceptance of God's Light.

Let us view surrender as a muscle. By taking exercise we develop our muscles. If we exercise every day, our muscles become strong, stronger, strongest. Surrender also grows by regular exercise. We can develop this surrender day by day. In one day we cannot make complete surrender to God. It is impossible. Nobody on earth has done such a thing. It is not your fault; it is not my fault; it is nobody's fault. But in order to achieve absolute surrender we have to exercise this spiritual quality constantly.

A perfect combination
Of prayer and surrender:
"Not my will, but Thine.
Let Thy Will be done."

Uniqueness I see in others. That means God has already blessed me with His fulness.

God wants all human beings—all His creations—to have an individuality of their own. Creation is such that in God's manifestation, no two human beings are alike. Not even two of our fingers are alike: one is shorter, one is longer. In His creation, God wants to enjoy Himself in infinite ways. No two beings are the same. So we should not be a carbon copy of anyone else.

Go beyond, farther beyond!
Do not limit yourself
By comparing yourself with others,
Or even with your own self.

As soon as you have conquered a difficulty, you will find that it repeats itself on a higher and subtler level. It is the same essential weakness in yourself which you are made to face in a more refined form.

You had hundreds of difficulties before you accepted the spiritual life. Under ordinary circumstances they would come to you one at a time. But if you accept the spiritual life, the inner life, God is most gracious in bringing all these difficulties right in front of you at once. At the same time He showers His special Grace on you so that all the difficulties may be overcome sooner. And what actually happens to our limitations, imperfections and ignorance? These are lions and tigers within us that we have been feeding. These tigers and lions are our desires, our wants that we have been feeding all the time. With God's Grace, they disappear.

Be cheerful!
You will get a lion's strength.
Immediately you will be able
To throw aside the burden of your past:
The elephant of depression,
Frustration and failure.

Difficulties indicate the strength of unwanted forces. Endurance indicates the inevitable victory of the soul's ever-fulfilling, ever-glowing light.

If we go deep within, we shall see that ninety-nine percent of the difficulties that we are now facing after accepting the spiritual life, we had before we accepted the spiritual life. At that time we were not conscious of them. But now that we have become conscious, we are aware of the difficulties that rise to fight against us. We should be glad not only that we have become conscious, but also that there is somebody, there is some higher factor—God and His miraculous Grace—who is more than eager to help us. As we become conscious, we realise Him. So we are most fortunate to be conscious of the difficulties that we have and we must never try to avoid them. We must accept them and know that with us, for us and in us is the omnipotent Grace of God.

Life is a constant battle
Because
God wants us to be
Supreme heroes.

If pleasure is a sheer dream, then pain is also a dream, a mere dream.

As long as we are in the physical, if our consciousness is all the time in the physical, there is pain. But if we can withdraw our consciousness from the physical, then there can be no pain. If you can consciously enter into the pain itself and stay in the pain for a few minutes, then the pain does not torture you as pain. For when we become the possessors of the pain, we can transform this very pain into joy. When you enter into the pain, you become the possessor of the pain. Right now, the pain possesses you; you are a victim of the pain and it keeps torturing you. But if you can possess the pain, you can actually inject into the pain anything that you want. With your conscious power, you can inject delight, joy or whatever you want.

If you claim to be
An Olympic seeker,
How can you bow before pain,
How?
Unbelievable!
Impossible!

FEBRUARY

Only one thing to learn in life:
You must think of yourself
The way God thinks of you—
As another God.

When I am all humility, I neither underestimate nor overestimate my life. What I do is to judge my life exactly the way my Lord Supreme judges my life.

Humility is the sweetest, softest, mildest and at the same time most fertile ground in us. Look at Mother-Earth. Can there be anybody or anything as humble as Mother-Earth? Mother-Earth is holding us, receiving all impacts from us, guiding us. She is all love, all compassion and at the same time, all powerful. But when we look at Mother-Earth, the first thing that comes to our mind is humility. We see this when we appreciate nature and natural beauty all around us. How humble they are! The more humble one is, the greater is his strength.

If you are planning to run
To Heaven,
First conquer your proud mind
With your humility-heart.

God is not something to be obtained from outside. God is that very thing which can be unfolded from within.

What do we mean by the spiritual life? We mean a life of inspiration, aspiration and inner communion. When you are able to meditate for a few minutes, the mind does not become a victim to doubts, impure thoughts and unhealthy ideas. If you really and truly accept the spiritual life, you will see that in the twinkling of an eye, most of your difficulties not only decrease but disappear. This happens because in your spiritual life there is abundant strength which you do not have in your outer life. This abundant strength, when it comes to the fore, makes the outer life surrender automatically to the inner life. And when it surrenders, it is not from compulsion, but from a spontaneous inner feeling. It surrenders with joy because it feels that in surrender itself, it gets the full power and total bliss of the inner life.

What you need every day
Early in the morning
Is a few quiet and self-giving moments
With God.

Adversity makes you dynamic. Adversity forces your eyes wide open. Adversity teaches you the meaning of patience. Adversity endows you with faith in yourself. Adversity opens the secret door through which you can see the ultimate future fulfilment of God's Will.

Let us not concern ourselves with frustration and suffering. Yes, they are here, but let us try to bring down God's Grace. If He Himself wants to carry our frustration, we will be making ourselves happy. Even if God does not take our pain, we can still let the flow of His Grace and Compassion descend into us. Then immediately it will illumine all our suffering, frustration and adversity.

You can face the world each day
If you pray and discuss with God
Your own life-problems
Early in the morning.

To endure the buffets of life firmly and calmly is to have the full taste of matchless equanimity.

Suffering we shall not invite, far from it. But if it comes, we have to see in it the existence of God. If we do not separate God from the suffering, then our own life-breath and God's Compassion will meet together. Otherwise we are not allowing God's Compassion to touch our life-breath, we are not seeing God's existence in everything. We say that God is everywhere. If God is everywhere, is He not also in suffering? Is God not in frustration? Is God so weak that He has to be only in Heaven and not in our painful, earth-bound existence? When we suffer, God is there. We have to see His Face and not the face of the suffering that tortures us. If we can do that, if we can see God's Face in everything, then we will see that suffering and frustration cannot exist. They have to be transformed into joy, constant joy, because our sweet Father, our affectionate, compassionate Father, is there in everything to protect us and save us.

Do not avoid
But transform
The things that need
Transformation.

The transformation of human nature in its completeness must unavoidably progress at the speed of a tortoise.

The world is full of competition. In the ordinary life, we are constantly competing. I am competing with you; you are competing with me. All the time, we are competing. But this competition must not take place in the spiritual life. In the inner life, there is no competition. It is only you and God. If there is any competition, let it be between you and your ignorance.

Each time you stumble,
Get up!
Then smile and walk
Slowly, steadily and unerringly
Along the aspiration-road.

You will make the fastest progress with the help of two things: God's Compassion-Eye and your enthusiasm-mind.

How fast can you leave aside your ignorance and go toward your own Goal? Competition, if it is at all necessary, should be to see how far behind us we have left ignorance and imperfection and how fast we are running towards our Goal. Let there be two sides: one, perfection's side; the other, imperfection's side. How fast are we running from imperfection and ignorance towards the positive side of perfection, truth, light and bliss? That, and not rivalry with others, should be our competition.

Your goal is not here;
It is far beyond.
Do not relax
Or lose your enthusiasm.
God wants you to run
An ultramarathon every day
To reveal the amazing capacity
Of a God-seeker-runner.

From time immemorial, history has been dealing with tyrants and liberators. Before long, it will have to deal seriously with peacemakers.

There are two wars, the inner and the outer. The inner war is the war that our inner being or the soul fights against limitations, ignorance, doubt and death. The outer war is the war that man fights with man, nation fights with nation. The question is: when and how can these wars come to an end? The outer war can come to an end only if the inner war stops first. That is to say, when the inner being or the soul conquers ignorance, fear, doubt and death, then in the outer world there will be no necessity to wage war. We fight because deep inside us there is disharmony, there is fear, there is anxiety and there is aggression. When deep within us there is peace, joy, plenitude and fulfilment, we shall not invite war. The outer war will come to an end when the inner war is resolved. Both wars will come to an end and are bound to end in the process of human evolution.

The inner experience of peace
Is man's supreme necessity.
The inner experience of peace
Is man's transcendental beauty.
The inner experience of peace
Is man's absolute reality.

Liberation means freedom from fear, freedom from doubt, freedom from ignorance and freedom from death.

As soon as you come into this world, you become prey to ignorance, fear, limitation and doubt. But through our spiritual practice and by living the inner life, we enter into the consciousness of the Divine. There we start growing, and a day comes when we become fully established in the spiritual consciousness of the inner life. Now we are caught by ignorance, we are wallowing in the pleasures of ignorance; but a day will dawn when we will be totally free from ignorance, and the moment we are free from ignorance, we will be liberated for good.

God created aspiration for you.
Can you not create determination
For yourself
So that your God-given aspiration
And your own determination
Can destroy your darkness-life forever?

Prepare yourself anew each day for your Supreme Lord's arrival with your heart's soulful prayer and your life's peaceful meditation.

One can be completely surrendered to God and still be responsible to worldly needs, but to worldly needs only according to God's Light. If God feels the need is a real need, that need can easily be fulfilled. Imaginary needs and demands are countless, but our true inner need is only one: illumination. If illumination is someone's real need, naturally God will fulfil that real need.

Knock at your own heart-door
To see God and feel God.
Knock at God's Heart-Door
To enter into His Heart-Room
And to sit there
With utmost joy, love and gratitude.

A self-controlled man smiles and smiles at the in-rushing of wild temptation.

Man, in his outer life or his outer achievements, is very limited. But the same man, when he enters into the inmost recesses of his heart, feels that there is something constantly trying to expand itself. This is consciousness. This consciousness links him with the Highest Absolute. Consciousness always welcomes us. It is in consciousness that we invoke, receive and offer boundless peace, light and bliss. An ordinary man does not have control of his consciousness. But a spiritual man is able to control his. He tries to lead a better life, a higher life, and in so doing, he brings down the light of the Beyond into the darkness of the present-day world.

The spiritual ladder has many rungs.
Now you are standing
On the sincerity-rung.
But if you do not step up
To the determination-rung,
How will you ever ascend?

To sail my life's danger-seas, I invite my peace-friend to help me in my boat.

Peace is based on love: love for humanity and love for God. Peace is also founded on non-attachment. No thirst for gain, no fear of loss—lo, peace is yours. Peace is also based on renunciation. This renunciation is not the renunciation of worldly possessions, but of limitation and ignorance. That peace is true peace which is not affected by the roaring of the world, outer or inner.

If you can love God
And manifest God
All the time in His own way,
Then God Himself will grant you
His own impenetrable
Peace-delight-armour.

The life of the ego and material success will eventually fail. The life that disciplines itself, the life that has a higher call, an inner call, can serve mankind most fruitfully. Devoted service to God is the real life.

Let us accept the inner life, the spiritual life. Mistakes in our journey are inevitable. Success without endeavour is impossibility itself. No work, no progress. Experience we must welcome, for we can learn nothing without experience. Experience may be either encouraging or discouraging. But it is experience that shows us the true meaning of our very existence.

My Lord,
Now that I am accepting
My defeats and my failures
As part of Your Cosmic Vision-Plan,
I am exceedingly happy.

If you start with your heart's aspiration-dawn, then you are bound to enjoy your soulful life's progress-day.

An unaspiring human being thinks that his ignorant pleasure-life is the only source of his satisfaction. But for sincere seekers, for true lovers of God, delight is the source. Beauty is light and light is delight. This delight is the harmony, peace and satisfaction of the Absolute. We can treasure this divine wealth only when we appreciate, admire and adore the inner beauty. When the inner beauty comes to the fore, the world of darkness will immediately be transformed into the world of luminosity.

If you can enjoy
Your heart's soulful meditation
And your life's fruitful action,
Then know and feel
That God is gloriously fulfilled
In and through you.

Perfection is the conscious annihilation of one's egocentric self.

How is it that a man does not know himself, something which ought to be the easiest of all his endeavours? He does not know himself precisely because he identifies himself with the ego and not with his real self. What compels him to identify himself with this pseudo-self? It is ignorance. And what tells him that the real self is not and can never be the ego? It is his self-search. What he sees in the inmost recesses of his heart is his real self, his God. Eventually this seeing must transform itself into becoming.

Do you not see?
Inside your heart
Somebody is continuously
Praying and meditating.
Can you not feel?
The divine Heartbeat
Of the Supreme Beloved
Is constantly beating within you.

Is God a dream? So does the human mind think. Is God a reality? So does the divine heart feel.

The Kingdom of Heaven is something that we can feel, and not something that we can demonstrate. Science can demonstrate many things. But the Kingdom of Heaven is a matter of our own inner achievement. If we have realised the Kingdom of Heaven within ourselves, others will look at us and feel that we have something quite unusual, unearthly and supernal. Because we have seen and felt and possessed the Kingdom of Heaven within ourselves, they will regard us as a totally transformed, extraordinary being.

If you want to inspire
The outer world,
Secretly aspire
In the inner world.

Increase, always increase your aspiration-cry. If you allow your aspiration to decrease, it will be your real disgrace.

It is our aspiration, our mounting inner cry, that leads us to this Kingdom of Heaven. The Kingdom of Heaven is a plane full of peace and delight. We feel it when we reside deep within ourselves and when we transcend our egocentric individual consciousness. The higher we go beyond our limited consciousness, the quicker we enter into our deepest, infinite consciousness, the more intimately we shall see, feel and possess the Kingdom of Heaven within ourselves.

Faith is the art of seeing
Without looking.
Aspiration is the art of becoming
Without hesitating.

Be universal in your love. You will see the universe to be the picture of your own being.

Complete and total perfection will come about only when we feel that our perfection is no perfection as long as the rest of humanity remains imperfect. If we call ourselves children of God, then others are also children of God. If we do not share with them what little we have, then what right have we to call them our brothers? They may be travelling a few miles behind us, or they may be fast asleep. But they must reach the Goal before perfect perfection can dawn on earth.

You are aspiring.
That means you are lifting up
The consciousness
Of those who are around you.

Perfection means living, spontaneous, constant oneness with the Inner Pilot.

Why is it that we are still imperfect? We are imperfect precisely because we do not cry for perfection in ourselves. We demand, or at least expect, infinitely more perfection in others than in ourselves. He and she are imperfect, and I am trying to perfect them, we say. But is it not absurd on my part to criticise and try to perfect others when I myself am imperfect? In this we make a Himalayan blunder. If we are sincere enough, we will realise that we spend too much time thinking of others. It is good to think of others, but not with our criticising, jealous, unlit mind. If we think of others with our soul's light, our soul's oneness, then automatically we are running toward perfection.

Who is the real loser?
He who enjoys
The superiority-inferiority-game.

Man's attachment to man binds man. Man's devotion to God liberates man.

Nobody can be as happy as a man who has detachment. We are under the impression that a man can be happy only when he is attached to something or to someone, but this is a great mistake. When we are attached to something or someone, we actually become a victim of that person or that thing. So in this world, if we want to have true joy, true peace and true divine qualities, then we must be totally detached. This detachment does not mean that we shall not work for the world; no, we shall have to work for the world, in the world, but we should not allow ourselves to be caught by anything.

My Lord Supreme,
Let me no longer play the game
Of attachment.
I wish only to play the game
Of devotedness—
To You, to You and to nobody else.

What are the laws of the universe? Love and serve. Love humanity. Serve Divinity.

I wish to tell you that there is nothing wrong with the world, but everything is wrong with you and me and the rest of the human beings. The poor world has not done anything wrong; it is we who are misusing the world. God has created this world; we are utilising the world. We can use it in our own way or in God's way. We can either destroy it or we can manifest the Divine here on earth. This world is the field of manifestation where we can manifest our inner divine qualities. At the same time, instead of manifesting the divine qualities deep within us, if we want to destroy the world, it is up to us. Let us take the world as an instrument. If we play the wrong note, then who is responsible? The player, not the instrument. If we use the world in a divine way, then we shall see that there is no problem with the world. It is we who have the capacity to use the world in a divine way and to fulfil the Divine here on earth.

Do not
Blame the world.
Find a solution.

By discriminating, by separating the true and eternal from the false and transient, I come to a point where I can see my Goal. Then I step upon the path leading to my Goal.

In our day-to-day life, if we want to emphasise our duty, then there is no end to our ordinary duties. We have to eat, we have to meet our friends, we have to see our family, we have to work. All kinds of duties we have. But we have to know that beyond these duties there is our real duty. These mundane duties we are fulfilling daily, but they do not bring us in any way nearer our Goal. There is only one Goal for each human being and that Goal is God-realisation. This does not mean that in order to realise God, we have to discard humanity. Far from it. We do not have to throw away the members of the family: wife, sisters, brothers, parents, children. No. We have to see in them the existence of God. This is one of the major duties of each human being, to see the existence of God in children, in friends, in everybody on earth.

I know you are busy.
At least, your mind has made you think so.
Even so, can you not find some time
To invite God, your Supreme Guest,
To bless you—your heart and your life—
With His all-illumining and all-fulfilling Presence?

God will make you one with Him if you know the meaning of silence.

You have to work on your inner life in your outer life's silence. No matter how divine, how significant or momentous your words, talking will have to surrender to silence. When you do not talk to anyone, this is the outer silence. But you also have to practise the inner silence. For inner silence, the mind must not talk either. In order to have inner silence, you have to silence the mind. The mind has to become calm and quiet, a sea of tranquility. Without this inner silence you cannot make any satisfactory progress in the inner life. There are many people who observe outer silence. This outer silence is good, but it cannot lead you very far unless and until you have established inner silence.

Only a purity-heart
Is permitted to pray
In the soul's silence-temple.

Love is the only wealth that man absolutely needs. Love is the only wealth that God precisely is.

Hate is an obverse form of love. You hate someone whom you really wish to love, but whom you cannot love. Perhaps he himself prevents you. That is a disguised form of love. You can only hate someone whom you have the capacity to love, because if you are really indifferent, you cannot even get up enough energy to hate him. Hatred is the frustration or blockage of normal, free-flowing love.

I cannot tell about others,
But I do know
That God will be there
To cheer for you
When you love His creation
Unconditionally.

In our spiritual life, there is only one enemy, a mighty enemy, and that is doubt.

We are always doubting. Either we are doubting ourselves or we are doubting God. In both cases, we limit ourselves. If we doubt ourselves, we can never realise God, and if we doubt God, then there is only frustration and misery in our life. If we have implicit faith in God, then this will be complemented by faith in ourselves. If we have faith in ourselves, then when we go deep within, we see that divine love is embracing us. If we have faith in ourselves, we can solve all our problems. This faith is not the arrogant pride of self-attachment, but the spontaneous light of wisdom.

Your doubtful mind
Has already challenged you.
It is up to you
Either to ignore its challenge
Or to destroy its volcano-attack.

Do you want to follow God? If you want to follow God, forget the human in you and ask the divine in you to possess you.

Grow with one thought: "God wants me and I need God." There should be no other thought around you. Then you will see that slowly, steadily and gradually, God's divine thoughts are entering into you and permeating your whole inner and outer existence. Then you will have tranquility in your body, in your vital, in your mind.

If your seeker-heart
Is flooded with hope,
God will definitely come to you
With a Liberation-Smile.

We offer our surrendered helplessness to God from below. He showers Blessings on us from above.

We cannot give to God anything more than He has given us. If He has given me a voice to sing, I will give Him my voice. If He has given me the capacity to dance, I will dance and please Him. If He has given me the capacity to write poems, then through poems I shall please Him. He has given me a divine gift, and it is I who have to offer what I have back to Him. Nothing do we create on our own. He gave us everything and with our deepest gratitude, we are offering Him what He first gave. So what we have and what we are, if we can consciously give to God, God will be most pleased.

If God wants you to manifest His Light
In a certain way,
Rest assured He will provide you
With the necessary opportunities.

The reward of faith and humility is always glory, founded upon the seeker's soulful oneness with God.

Always try to feel that you are the chosen child of the Supreme just because He is utilising you. If you feel that you are utilising yourself with your own ego and pride, then you are thousands of miles away from God. The moment you are away from Him, you have to feel that you are nothing, you are useless. The moment you are one with Him with your dedication, devotion and surrender, you will feel that you are everything. When you feel that you are everything, automatically your receptivity expands.

Awareness is the only thing
That my mind needs.
Soulfulness is the only thing
That my heart needs.
Oneness—my constant, sleepless,
Inseparable oneness with my Lord Supreme—
Is the only thing that I need.

Always try, during your meditation, during your conscious life, to feel that you are God's chosen child, God's pride.

God needs us to fulfil Him, to manifest Him. We can say, "God needs me; thus I have surrendered. I have to fulfil God on earth because God wants it, not because I want it. God wants me to realise Him, to fulfil Him on earth. What more do I need?" That should be the only concern for a spiritual aspirant. And in that concern everything is covered. All problems are solved, all answers are given when we feel that God wants us, God needs us for His manifestation on earth.

He is really something!
He has learned the supreme secret
Of tirelessly working
For the divine manifestation
Without receiving or demanding
Any outer recognition.

MARCH

If you travel all the time
On the wings of hope,
And not
On the wings of determination,
You are not going to succeed
In the battlefield of life.

He who loves never grows old. God is a shining example.

You may feel that in this world, some people are very bad. But by feeling that a person is very bad or by hating that person, are you gaining anything? That particular person has not gained anything from your hatred. And what have you done? By hating that person, you have lost something very sweet in yourself. Why should one lose something very precious of her own, just because she wants to correct someone by hating him? In this world, we have to be very wise. You will say that he is very bad and that you have to do something. But hating is not the right instrument. If you want to use the right weapon, the most effective weapon will be love.

Your mind knows only
How to compile complaints.
Your heart knows only
How to sing oneness-song.

Pray to God to grant you the same love that He uses to love Himself, so that you can enjoy freedom infinite from your earth-bound ego-fetters.

You may think that love is not a strong enough weapon, whereas hatred is like a sharp knife. No. The power of love is infinitely more powerful than the power of hatred, because when you love someone, at that time his divine qualities have to come forward. Someone has done something nasty to you. But now what do you want? You want to punish him and strike him? After striking him, what will happen? In you, there is something called a conscience. That conscience will prick you. You will say, "What have I done? He has done something wrong, true, but now I have done something worse. Then in which way am I superior to him?" You can develop love daily if early in the morning, when you get up, you pray to God, "O God, in Your creation I want to see only good qualities in others. If bad qualities are around me, or if people are bothering me, then please give me the necessary patience so that I can remain full of peace in my outer life. People may have done wrong things to me, but let me offer them my patience."

Patience
Is at once
God and man's
Sacred victory-secret.

Self-confidence means God's inner guidance.

In the spiritual life, God gives us the capacity to do what He wants. Our surrender to Him is our way of helping ourselves, because He gives us the right attitude and tells us the kind of action that should take place in the outer world. God's Power and God's Light give us the capacity to help ourselves. We have to make an effort, but we must all the time remember that God is our Source. It is He who is giving us the capacity to help ourselves. We have to be His instruments. We do the work, but we have to do it for God. You are God's child and He will fulfil all your needs. Just as you fulfil your own child's needs, God will fulfil your needs.

If you do not obey
The whispering of your soul,
Yours will be a life
Of bitter frustration.

First be an illumined individual. Then you can become the creator of a fulfilled world.

It is through the inner world that our outer world can be fulfilled. As you sow within, so shall you reap without. If early in the morning I offer to God one divine thought, one spiritual thought, I will see that during the day I receive the fruits of that divine thought. If I pray for or meditate on divine love, joy or peace, during the day I will enjoy the fruits of my prayer and meditation in the form of love, joy, peace or whatever I am crying for. The inner world can and must affect the outer world—for the better.

What you powerfully hold
In your thought-world
Will make you either
A street beggar
Or a great king.

If you are leading a spiritual life, then at every moment, God comes first in your life.

To an ordinary person, God does not come first. Prosperity, power, importance, fame and other things come first. But a spiritual person says, "God has to come first; the inner life has to come first." As we sow, so we reap. We sow a seed and it germinates. Then it grows into a huge banyan tree. So our inner life must come first because everything in our outer life, whether or not it is spiritual, is a result and an embodiment of our inner life. A spiritual person feels that the inner life is of paramount importance and that it has to come first. An ordinary person feels, "No, the spiritual life is vague and meaningless. Let us enjoy life. Let us possess and be possessed. Let us enjoy the world and let the world enjoy us. There is no bridge between the spiritual life and the ordinary life." But a spiritual person sincerely cries, "Let me realise the Truth in its own way and then bring down the Truth into my outer life." The Truth is within, but it has to be felt and expressed outwardly also.

Unless you put God first
In everything you do and say,
Your aspiring life
Will wither away to nothingness.

First pray to God devotedly to claim you as His very own. Then only will you be able to claim the world as your very own.

The more we follow the inner life, the more meaningful will be the outer life. Otherwise, the outer achievement without the core, that is to say, without the inner life, will have no meaning. Nothing will satisfy you or me or anybody on earth except the inner life. The inner life is the life of the soul, where reality and divinity are constantly growing. So please follow the inner life, and the inner life will guide you, inspire you, instruct you on how you can be divinely and supremely successful in your outer life.

You just sail
Your aspiration-boat.
God will broadcast
Your supreme adventure-glories.

Think less and meditate more. Plan less and act more.

Meditation will free you from the sea of ignorance. Meditation will give you everlasting freedom. And this freedom is the freedom of oneness. Right now you cannot unite yourself even with another person right beside you. You feel with your ego that you are yourself and she is somebody else. So where is freedom? With your very limited capacity and limited knowledge you are trying to exercise your will and utilise your human power to lord it over others. That is what you call freedom. This is not freedom. Real freedom is inseparable oneness with the universe. You are growing together. You are achieving something and you are seeing that the entire world is achieving it at the same time.

The present way
Is not the way to become good.
The present way
Is not the way to love God's creation.
The way to become good
Is to pray sleeplessly.
The way to love God's creation
Is to meditate unconditionally.

A poor mind complains. A rich heart maintains its oneness all the time with God the creation.

If you want inner freedom, spiritual freedom, then I wish to say that it is in becoming one with the rest of humanity. From the freedom that you cherish by separating yourself from others, what are you gaining? Yes, we should separate ourselves from ignorance, imperfection, limitation, bondage and so forth, but we should not and we must not separate ourselves from our soul, from the reality which is light and delight. When we are following the spiritual life, we have to know that our real freedom is in identifying ourselves with the rest of the world, with humanity at large. By becoming one, we stand united, we march united toward the Highest. United we shall fulfil our Goal.

My Lord Supreme,
Do give me the capacity
To love the body-reality of Your creation
In exactly the same way
That I have been loving
The Soul-Immortality of Your Vision.

Your inner existence and God's outer reality are one.

When you divinely love yourself, not emotionally or egotistically, you are loving yourself just because God is breathing inside you, because God wants to fulfil Himself through you. If you love yourself egotistically, you are killing yourself. If you love yourself undivinely, you are binding yourself. But when you love yourself divinely, you love yourself just because inside you is God. That is why you are loving yourself. You and God are one.

I shall bid you to do
The right thing:
Love yourself sincerely and soulfully.
I shall forbid you to do
The wrong thing:
Cherish no low opinion of yourself
And rest not foolishly with indolence.

Do not waste your God-service hours thinking mundane thoughts.

Complaining can never be of any use. Every time we make a complaint, we limit ourselves and bind ourselves. Our life of aspiration is self-expansion for God-manifestation. If complaints start, they are our veritable enemies. Each complaint is an enemy, a fall, a descent from the all-loving and all-embracing reality-tree of which we are the loving, illumining and fulfilling fruits.

If you live in an atmosphere
Of aspiration,
Perfection will be
Your God-given name.

If your meditation is truly high and deep, then you are bound to have a silent dialogue with peace.

The way to find inner peace is to meditate on the heart, where there is constant joy, constant love. At that time we will not cry for appreciation from others. We will depend on our inner Source, where there is infinite joy, infinite love, infinite peace.

Do not give up,
Do not give up!
Your prayer-life
Is your future salvation.
Your meditation-heart
Is your future perfection.
Do not give up!

Every action of ours should be to please God and not to gain applause. Our actions are too secret and sacred to display before others. They are meant for our own progress, achievement and realisation.

In order to be conscious of God during our day-to-day activities, we have to feel that each action we perform is equally important in God's Eye. We have to act with a surrendered attitude, with pure thoughts and an illumined mind. If we act to satisfy our ego, vanity or pride, then we can never be conscious of the divinity within, then we cannot be conscious of our true existence in our outer life. God has a special mission for each of us and our soul has taken incarnation to manifest this mission. We have to feel that we have a divine purpose, a divine goal.

Your heart has come into the world
To work for God
And not to be worshipped by man.

Love God, only God, unreservedly—if possible, unconditionally.

Love. Whom are you loving? You are loving the Supreme in each individual. When you love the body, you bind. When you love the soul, you free yourself. It is the soul in the individual, it is the Supreme in each human being that you love. Nothing can be greater than love. God is great only because He is infinite Love. If one wants to define God, one can define Him in millions of ways; but I wish to tell you that no definition of God can be as adequate as saying, "God is all Love." If fear comes into our mind when we say "God," then we are millions and billions of miles away from God. When we repeat the name of God, if love comes to the fore, then our prayers, our concentration, our meditation and our contemplation are genuine.

Just love God a little more;
Just think of yourself a little less.
Lo and behold,
All your untold problems are solved.

Conceal your nervousness; you will eventually die. Reveal your nervousness; you will eventually be the conqueror.

The whole world is captured by restlessness and nervousness. The very aim of practising yoga is to have peace, peace of mind. When one acquires peace of mind, automatically one possesses indomitable inner strength. How can nervousness enter into a person when he is surcharged with inner strength? There can be no restlessness, no nervousness. Nervousness comes when you take away a part from the whole. Fear comes when you separate something from the whole. God is the whole. God is the Absolute. When you practise yoga, you touch the Absolute and enter into the Absolute; you do not remain a separate portion of the whole. When you enter into the Absolute, there is all strength, all power; there is no fear. In yoga you can cure all nervousness, all restlessness and all imperfection.

Say to your doubting mind, "No!"
Say to your loving heart, "Yes!"
You will be relieved
From your nervous tension.

In case you have not noticed, there is an inevitable link between the human desire-life and ceaseless frustration-night.

No matter how well-grounded you are in the spiritual life, you will see that in attachment there is only frustration. In attachment, if your desires are not fulfilled, immediately frustration comes in. In the spiritual life, we must end all attachments. To be freed from attachment does not mean that you have to be cold, aloof and distant towards everyone. Attachment should be transformed into proper understanding and oneness. Attachment is not real oneness. Attachment exists often just for the moment; then, out of sight, out of mind. Real oneness with human beings is most important. In oneness we are never frustrated because oneness implies the strongest inner understanding, and this inner understanding is illumination.

If you sincerely want to free yourself
From attachment-jungle,
Then associate yourself with the seekers
Who have more faith in God
And more love of God
Than you have.

Think of others. Your heart will be pleased with you. Free others from your snare. Your God will be pleased with you.

How can we have detachment? It is through aspiration. Detachment does not mean completely cutting off all relationships. Detachment is the proper understanding of the truth at its own level. And in detachment, we will see that we are one with humanity on the strength of our inner life. We misunderstand and fear the word detachment because we feel that we are breaking something. No, we are not breaking. We are actually connecting ourselves properly in the inner world to other people with our illumining and fulfilling souls. This we do with aspiration. The more we aspire, the larger becomes our vision. And this vision is our real reality.

The grip of attachment may please me
For a fleeting second,
But
The grasp of detachment
Can surely and easily please me
For my entire life.

Meditate, meditate, meditate! Pay more attention to your meditation. Spend more time in meditation. Meditate soulfully, prayerfully and devotedly.

In this world, we do everything because we have a love for it. We do things for human beings, for our relatives, our children, because we love them. We acquire skills because we have a keen interest in them. If we feel that we have a real love for meditation, then we can easily meditate. We have to grow within us a love for meditation. Meditation is not an object. It is a subject. We enjoy studying history because we have a love for knowing about the great events of the world and the great figures of history. Similarly, if we have a real love for God, then we will do the thing that is necessary to love Him. We will start meditating.

Just a quick reminder to meditate.
Meditate soulfully;
You will conquer ignorance-night
Easily.
Just a quick reminder to meditate.
Meditate unconditionally;
You will gain the Lord Supreme
Everlastingly.

If we constantly harbour good thoughts, divine thoughts, pure thoughts, then the negative forces cannot stay with us.

Every day, early in the morning, at least for five minutes, we have to exercise our positive thought, positive will, positive force. What do we mean by positive force? We mean that the Truth exists within us and is being realised. Then we try to feel that the Truth is already embodied. Finally we try to feel that the Truth has to be revealed and manifested in us and through us. Then there can be no negative force to disturb us or destroy our aspiration. Very often we allow the negative forces to attack us. If we do not give them the chance, then the negative forces have to remain thousands of miles away from us.

Just love the higher life more.
The lower life
Will automatically shun you.

God's Grace can and will blot out the past if and when you are ready to face and transcend the facts of your present life.

When we are doing something wrong, if we know that there is someone who has boundless Grace, boundless Compassion, then let us go to Him for rescue. But we also have to understand consciously that we should not do things that are wrong because the law of karma, the law of action, will call on us. If I go on doing wrong things, how can I expect a better life, a more fulfilling life? No. I have to pay for it. Every moment God has given me the chance either to do the right thing or, if I make friends with ignorance, to do the wrong thing. So it is up to me. If I do the right thing, naturally I will have God's Light, Peace, Bliss, Harmony and Perfection in my life, and if I do wrong, I have to pay the price exacted by the law of karma.

No experience is free
In the outer world.
No realisation is free
In the inner world.

Regard your earthly duties as divine duties. You will see that God is responsible for the fruit of your actions.

If you have surrendered to God all that you have and all that you are, then you can feel that God is responsible for all your activities. If you feel that you are responsible for your children, for your parents, for your friends, and if you feel that you have to kindle the flame of aspiration or illumine their unlit nature, then you are mistaken. You will not get peace for yourself nor will you be able to offer peace to any of God's children on earth. God is responsible; God is indispensable. You have to work soulfully, devotedly and unconditionally to see God in each human being at every moment. It is through conscious and constant surrender to the Will of God that you will be able to feel this.

Now that you have become
Your life's surrender-sunrise,
God is granting you
His Heart's Immortality-Sky.

When I think good thoughts, I feel that man is not, after all, so bad.

God has given us an intelligent mind. He has given us a sound body. He has given us a strong vital. He has given us many things to appreciate. He has given us receptivity. Let us fill our vessel full to the brim with good thoughts, divine thoughts. He has given us the potentiality, the possibility plus the opportunity to develop our good qualities. If we are really sincere, we will feel that God has given us blessings beyond our capacity—not only beyond our capacity, but beyond our necessity.

In the morning God blesses me
With pure motives.
In the afternoon God blesses me
With clear ideas.
In the evening God blesses me
With rare rewards.

By having a guilty consciousness, you do not get light or wisdom.

If you have done something that is not right, then try to do the right thing, the divine thing. This second, this minute you have used. You could have used it either for a right purpose or a wrong purpose. If you have used it for a wrong purpose, then use the following minute for a divine purpose. If you use this moment for a divine purpose without thinking of the previous minute when you did something wrong, then what happens? Your positive strength, the will-power you have used to do the right thing, will then have power in its entirety, in its fulness. But if you think of the past minute with a sense of guilt, that you have done something wrong, and then the following minute you are determined to do the right thing, half of your power is again lost in darkness and only half can be utilised for the right action. So, try to bring to the fore your full power in the following minute and nullify the previous mistake.

The sunlit way to realise God
Is to clearly forget
And wisely forgive
One's past failures.

Do not think of the past. Go forward with a silent mind and stay not where you are with your bondage-memories.

If one cherishes or broods over misdeeds, then one is again strengthening one's own guilt unconsciously. I may think, "I am repenting." But why should I repent? If I have done something wrong, then I have the capacity to do the right thing. By focusing all our attention on the right thing, we are adding to our positive strength. The sense of guilt, the constant feeling of self-reproach, is unfortunately all-pervading in the Western world. If my Source is God, the absolute infinite Light, if I know that it is from there that I came, then someday I must go back to my Source. During my stay on earth I got, unfortunately, some unhealthy, unaspiring and destructive experiences. Now I have to get rid of these unfortunate experiences. I have to get fulfilling experiences in my life. So for that I have to concentrate only on the right thing, the divine thing which will fulfil me, and not on the things that have stood in my way.

God's Compassion-Eye gives us
Not only one chance
But countless chances
To change our wrong directions.

Inside I love soulfully and sleeplessly. Outside I give generously and unconditionally.

When we look for the inner light, we do not have to give up the material life at all. We have to live on earth. If we give up the members of our family, our children, our parents and our dear ones, then tomorrow we will give up the inner life also. Then what are we going to get? Where is God? God is inside everyone. Now, what are we going to give up? We are going to give up ignorance. We are going to give up bondage. We are going to give up temptation, our own temptation and other undivine things. But if we say that we have to give up our earthly existence in order to realise God, then it is a mistake. It is not required at all. God is here on earth as He is in Heaven.

Keep your inner life sacred
And not secret.
Keep your outer life soulful
And not powerful.

If you want God, you have to live a simple life.

There are only twenty-four hours in the day, and when they are gone, they do not come back again. If you waste an hour, then it is lost to you forever. You will not be able to retrieve it. You have to decide what you will use each fleeting moment for—for worldly pleasure, or for God. If you feel that your first and foremost necessity is God, then if you simplify your life, you will not be distracted or tempted. If you keep all the objects of temptation around you, then you are consciously and deliberately delaying your spiritual progress.

If you are meant to do something great
For God,
Then the desire-life is not meant
For you.

Any method of spiritual discipline will have two inevitable and inseparable wings: absolute patience and firm resolution.

If I have to choose which quality is most important and fulfilling at the beginning of the spiritual life, then I must say that it is self-discipline. What we need is a disciplined life. Our mind is a victim to doubt, worries, anxieties and so forth. A disciplined life will not have the same fate. It will have joy and peace. A disciplined life comes from constant practice. Nobody can be a world champion overnight. What does practice mean? Practice means patience. Patience is not something weak. It is something dynamic; it is something illumining. We need patience in order to have a disciplined life. Today, if we want to discipline our life all at once, it may be impossible. But tomorrow it will be possible.

To increase
My inner progress-delight,
I have renewed my attention
To the self-discipline-life.

If you can silence the mind and ask the heart to speak to God, then only are you heading in the right direction.

Meditation is like an inner flashlight. When you enter into a dark room with a flashlight, immediately the room is illumined. When we enter with our meditation into our subconscious, unconscious, or even inconscient parts, immediately we feel that light has dawned. And when the light dawns, immediately the divinity, which is the silence within us, gets the opportunity for universal expansion.

Every day
Pray to the Lord Supreme
To bring to the fore
Your inner sun.
It will silence
Your mind's confusion-candle.

A life of beauty is a life of peace.

Peace is not merely the absence of quarrelling and fighting; peace is the manifestation of our inseparable oneness with all. This oneness is not the oneness of the finite with the finite, but the oneness of the finite with the Infinite. When the finite identifies itself with the Infinite, the beauty of the Infinite transforms the very breath of the finite, and earth's beauty and Heaven's beauty are joined. Earth's beauty is a soulful cry; Heaven's beauty is a soulful smile. When earth's cry and Heaven's smile meet together, beauty's perfection dawns.

When my peace-heart
Dreams,
My bliss-life
Sings.

A disciplined life can come from only one thing, and that is aspiration, our inner cry.

When you cry for outer things, sometimes you get them, sometimes you do not. But if your inner cry is sincere, you will see that the fulfilment dawns. A child cries for milk. He is crying in his cradle in the living room. The mother may be in the kitchen. Wherever she is, when she hears his cry, the mother comes running to feed the child with milk. Why? The mother feels the cry of the child is genuine and sincere. Similarly, in the spiritual life we have an inner cry. If we have that inner cry, then it does not matter when we cry. It may be at one o'clock or at three o'clock or at noon, in the morning or in the evening. At any hour, that inner cry reaches God, and God is bound to fulfil that inner cry.

Never permit
Your heart's streaming tears
To evaporate.
Never!

In the silence of your heart, your life's perfection cannot remain a far cry.

If one wants to discipline himself, if one is dissatisfied with his life, and if he feels that from a disciplined life he can have real fulfilment, perfection and satisfaction, then God is bound to help that particular sincere seeker. If there is an inner cry, then nothing on earth can be denied. No fulfilment can be denied to an individual who has an inner cry.

God's Compassion-Light
Is never discouraged,
No matter how bad I was yesterday,
No matter how useless I am today,
For it knows that I embody
His Cosmic Vision's
Perfection-manifestation-promise.

Controlling desire is good. Better is non-attachment. Best it is to feel oneself removed from the snare of nature.

There is a great difference between pleasure and joy. The human world, the outer consciousness, is crying for pleasure and each time pleasure is fulfilled, we see that frustration looms large in pleasure. But if we feel that joy is coming into our lives, then joy grows from joy into more joy, abundant joy, boundless joy. When we meditate for five minutes or ten minutes, we get inner joy that fulfils us. When we think of buying something unnecessary like a Cadillac or something of that sort, we are fulfilling our pleasure. Soon after, we are frustrated because the one we have got is not big enough, we want something more comfortable. If we run after comfort with the help of our desire, then naturally we will not be satisfied. But if we cry for joy, inner joy, then each time we are running towards fulfilment, because inner joy wants us only to fulfil God; and only by fulfilling God can we be really fulfilled.

Unless you are always
Spiritually cautious,
You are bound to be washed away
By a flash flood of desire.

APRIL

Give and give and give!
Soon you will realise
That self-giving is not
A most difficult task.

Life needs and wants victory, but the victory that we achieve in the world of sound does not last for long. The victory that we achieve in the world of silence is everlasting.

Silence is preparation, our preparation for God's examination. We come to know God's Hour only when we observe silence, only when we dive deep within. An unaspiring person does not know and cannot know God's Hour. If God's Hour dawns in his life, he fails to notice it. But a seeker who practises silence every day for half an hour or an hour knows when God's Hour is going to strike. God not only tells him when the Hour will strike but also, like a private tutor, helps the seeker to pass his inner examination.

I give birth to thunder-noise
When I challenge the pride
Of ignorance-night.
I give birth to silence-voice
When I sleep in the heart
Of my aspiration-light.

Do not question and doubt the sorrows of the world. Question the sincerity of your self-investigation.

World-perfection is something very complicated. Perfection means satisfaction. For a seeker, satisfaction depends on his own inner progress. His inner progress depends on how much peace he has received and how many undivine things he has been able to discard from his outer life. Let him see how few things he can live with on earth. If he is a sincere, devoted and dedicated seeker, then his list will have only one item: God-satisfaction.

He who lives a simple, God-loving life
Is chosen by God Himself
To fight for Him
Against devouring ignorance-night.

Perfection is our inner and outer progress, and this inner and outer progress gives us boundless delight.

We are all seekers. So, for us, world-perfection is nothing but God-satisfaction. But we have to know that God-satisfaction will not take place in all of humanity all at once. No, it will take place in individuals, one by one. Today it will dawn in you, tomorrow it will dawn in somebody else and the day after tomorrow it will dawn in a third person. An individual starts his journey with his own life. He knows how much he has suffered from fear, doubt, worry and other undivine qualities. Then there comes a time when he sees that these qualities are very few in number and very limited in capacity. So he knows that he has made considerable progress. This progress is nothing but perfection in his life.

Make
Healthy choices.
Perfection
Will be yours.

My imperfect gift to God is yesterday, yesterday's experience. God's perfect gift to me is today, today's realisation.

Each individual will achieve perfection at God's choice Hour. It may not be today or tomorrow, but God has His own choice Hour for everyone. That choice Hour depends entirely on our inner progress. If we cry most sincerely, then we can expedite God's Hour. If it was to take place tomorrow, it can take place today. God's Hour entirely depends on our aspiration and inner cry. If our cry is intense, then God will accelerate our progress, which is our continuous perfection. World-perfection is bound to dawn at God's choice Hour.

As long as your heart
Feels the dew of hope,
God will appear before you
With His saving Grace.

Doubt is more to be disliked than death. Why? Because when you doubt yourself or God, it is the real beginning of your hastening end.

The human in us feels that we are either the lowest or the highest. When it identifies with the lowest, it says, "I am useless, I am nothing." In this way the vital comes forward and tries to gain sympathy. But each time a doubt comes and we feel that we are not God's instrument, we fall short of our capacity. How many times we doubt ourselves, belittle ourselves, kill ourselves! The moment we doubt that God is inside us, a dark spot appears on the golden tablet of our heart. When we do not love ourselves, the face of the sun is covered with clouds. The moment we belittle our capacity and doubt ourselves, the moment we forget what we eternally are, at that time we are millions of miles from the truth. We love ourselves only when we feel that we have achieved something or feel that tomorrow or the day after we are going to do something. This is the human in us.

Of what use is my achievement
If I have the fear
That tomorrow
Somebody will do better than I?

Doubt is the worst possible impurity in the human mind.

God is our highest part, our most illumined part. When we as individuals enter into our highest consciousness and know that we are in all, of all and for all, at that time we do not doubt ourselves. At that time, we are everything, so who can doubt whom? We embody God and want to reveal and manifest God, so we do not even dream of minimising our capacity. We are spontaneously embodying and revealing the divine. When the real, the highest, the most illumined part in us comes to the fore, at that time we really love ourselves. We love ourselves because we know who we are. Love is not a kind of outer movement or action. Love is life, and life itself is spontaneous nectar and delight. The Supreme in us, who is infinite delight, loves us infinitely more than we love ourselves.

My Lord,
Do teach me only one thing:
How to love the world
The way You love me.

Inner obedience is the conscious recognition of one's higher life, higher reality, higher existence.

Inner obedience is a supreme virtue. Inner obedience is the achievement of one's true knowledge. When we obey the higher principles, higher laws, we love. When we love, we become. And when we become, we come to realise that we eternally are the Eternal Now. We listen to the Inner Pilot, who is guiding our destiny, who is moulding and shaping us in His own way. A seeker always tries to obey his inner voice. But very often a wrong voice will create unimaginable problems for the seeker. How will the seeker differentiate the real from the unreal, the right from the wrong? A sincere seeker will be able to distinguish a wrong voice if he notices that the voice wants him to get satisfaction from its message in a specific way, with specific results. If the voice makes him feel that satisfaction will come only if victory dawns, if success comes, then he knows it is a wrong voice. When defeat looms large at the end of his action, and the seeker is doomed to disappointment, then he has to know it was a wrong voice. The right voice, the divine voice, will only inspire the seeker to right actions. The right voice does not care for results as such.

Each divine thought
That comes to you
Will come to you, without fail,
Like the sunrise.

Do not think of the result. Your sincere effort to serve God is what counts most. That in itself is the greatest achievement.

"You have the right to action but not to the fruits thereof." This is the message of the Bhagavad Gita. The fruits of action come either in the form of success or in the form of failure. But neither success nor failure is our ultimate aim. Our aim is progress. Today's success will pale into insignificance tomorrow. If we take life as a song of gradual progress, then life is a constant satisfaction. But if we see it in terms of success and failure, then immediately our patience will be exercised. Today we do not get one kind of success; tomorrow we try to get another kind of success. And we try to achieve this success by hook or by crook, using any means—foul or fair—because all we want is something to satisfy our immediate need. But our immediate need is not our eternal need. Our eternal need is for progress.

Today's failure-plants
Will tomorrow grow into
Success-trees.
Patience from below
And Compassion from above
Can and will do the impossible
Easily.

Aspiration burns away outer impurity and imperfection, while at the same time it clears up all that is disturbing our inner consciousness.

When the flame of aspiration has been kindled in you and is burning most effectively, you must allow it to blaze fully. You will see that the outer world, the disturbing world, is actually deep inside you. Then things that have to be transformed will then be transformed. There is no other way to fight outer disturbances than to keep the flame of aspiration burning constantly.

Meditate with greatest enthusiasm
If you want to make the fastest progress
In your aspiration-heart
And in your dedication-life.

Man, in essence, is not ugly. But hard is it for man to appear beautiful, for he has lost the contact with his soul, the child of All-Beauty.

If you can see the divine qualities in others—if you can see in each person a divine child, or a beautiful flower, or a burning candle symbolising the ascent of the flame of aspiration—you will be full of joy. If you see inside them somebody praying and meditating, or a most luminous, divine child, you will be full of joy. If you see the divine in a person, then your strength, inspiration and aspiration will increase. The moment you think that you see an undivine quality in someone else, feel that your whole hand is full of ink. You are soiled. You can wash it with a good thought. But if you touch the ink again, even though you have washed your hand once, it will again become dirty and black.

Each soulful thought
Is not only a life-cleaner
But also a God-distributor.

Each day is the renewal of life. Each day is the rebirth of our inner assurance that each individual is the chosen instrument of the Supreme to reveal and fulfil the infinite Divine here on earth.

If you do not look for the negative qualities in others, automatically the positive qualities come forward. It is like this: either you like a person or you dislike him. If you do not dislike someone, automatically you like him. It is either one or the other; there is nothing in between. At every moment the mind is either thinking of something positive and creative or of something negative and destructive. So the best thing is to see the positive things in others. If you consciously see the positive things, then the negative qualities cannot come forward.

Before your mind
Changes your thought,
You can send your thought
To change the world.

How can your heart be constantly flooded with aspiration-satisfaction, when you consciously allow your mind to be shrouded in dismal suspicions?

You should always listen to your higher part. Right now your mind is superior to your physical and your vital. When the mind asks you to do something, immediately the physical does it, the vital does it. But again, the heart is superior to the mind. The mind doubts and suspects; it does not have one-pointed aspiration for a particular goal, whereas the heart gets light and illumination from the soul. That is why the heart is superior.

Train your mind to obey you.
Train your life
To surrender to your heart.
Happiness will be your permanent property.

The greatest misfortune that can come to a human being is to lose his inner peace. No outer force can rob him of it. It is his own thoughts, his own actions, that rob him of it.

How can a person really find inner peace? On the practical level, do not expect anything from others on the physical plane. Just give and give and give, like a mother who gives everything to her child thinking that the child is not in a position to give her anything in return. Do not expect anything from the world; only love the world and offer your capacity, your inner wealth, your joy. Everything that you have, give to the world unconditionally. If we expect anything from the world, then we will feel miserable because the world does not understand us, the world does not care for us. So if we can do anything unconditionally, then we will have peace of mind.

To complete
The golden dream of peace,
Selflessly serve
And unconditionally love.

The highest knowledge is the knowledge of one's conscious, constant and, at the same time, ever-transcending oneness with the Inner Pilot.

If we have expectation, we will always be frustrated. We should act only because God wants us to do something. We should feel that we are His instruments and He is working in and through us. When we act or speak only to please God in His own way, without expectation, then only will we cease to experience frustration.

If you give God your heart's
Dearest treasure, surrender,
Then God will grant you His Vision's
Dearest treasure, peace.

We can be more conscious in our outer life only when we feel that the outer life has no existence without the inner life, the life of inner light. The inner life is the foundation. If the foundation is not solid, then the superstructure cannot be strong and permanent.

Early in the morning when the day dawns, we have to feel that God comes first in our life. For ten minutes or fifteen minutes or half an hour, we have to invoke God's presence. The presence of God is constant everywhere, but if we feel that God is someone else, somewhere else, then we have to invoke Him from the highest Heaven. If we feel that God is already within us but lying so deep that we cannot see or feel Him, then we have to pray to God to come to the fore. Either a seeker has to invoke God from without or he has to bring God's inner presence to the fore. Then, when he feels God's presence, he feels that his life is secure, for God's presence means God's infinite Power, infinite Light.

Unless you aspire,
You will always be compelled
To remain a prisoner
Of bewilderment.

To feel the absence of ego is as difficult as to see God's constant presence in oneself.

The desire-thief in us wants to be as vast as the ocean, but when somebody brings him in front of the ocean and tells him to jump into the ocean, he becomes frightened to death. If we aspire, at that time nobody will ever have to bring us in front of the sea. We ourselves will come and jump into the sea and start swimming. Ego makes us want to become something vast, but inner courage it does not have. When we have aspiration, we have inner courage. We know that we will not drown, but on the contrary, we will be illumined.

According to your heart's receptivity-smile,
God is trying and trying
To manifest Himself in and through you
In a very special way.

Although regularity in spiritual practice may appear mechanical, it is a constant blessing from above and shows the development of some inner strength.

We cannot meditate twenty-four hours a day. We have to go to work or to school. But while answering our boss's questions, we can feel the living presence of our inner being. We can feel the presence of a divine child, a divine presence guiding us. This inner feeling is surcharged with light, peace and bliss. How can we develop this inner feeling? It cannot happen overnight. It is like a muscle. To develop a muscle we must take exercise daily. In the spiritual life also if we practise daily, regularly, soulfully, we are bound to develop this inner capacity. Even if we speak about mundane things, we will not lose the inner wealth that we accumulated during our meditation early in the morning.

God does not expect from you
At the very beginning
Mastery in anything,
But He does expect from you
In everything
Your soulful willingness.

If you do the right thing, eventually you will inspire others to do the right thing.

We know that it is really difficult for us to make a little progress by ourselves in the spiritual life, in our inner life and in our outer life. So we have to have infinite patience in order to see a little transformation in human nature, that is to say, in mankind as a whole. We must not lose patience. Just because our neighbours and friends are not following the spiritual life, it does not mean that we should give up. We have to know that there was a time, either in this incarnation or in past incarnations, when we were also perhaps of their type or even worse. We have to try to help people with the idea that once upon a time we were also unaspiring, unspiritual, but then by God's Grace we became spiritual. Perhaps we may not be conscious of who actually helped us. But there was someone who helped us in our spiritual journey, in our inner awakening. So we shall also try to inspire people. If one person gets inspiration from us, that is enough.

How to inspire others
When inspiration deserts you?
Speak of the bright sunny days
Which you have seen countless times
Inside you.
Perhaps others have never had
Even one sunny day.

How can I be a better human being if I do not think of the Source?

Who makes you good? Who makes you better? Who makes you best? Somebody who is infinitely better than you are, and that is God. When the necessity arises from within, you can be a good human being; you can help other people. Now, who is supplying you with the inspiration and aspiration to help mankind? God. The moment you want to be a better human being, you have to offer your good qualities: your sincerity, your humility, your love for mankind. These good qualities come from only one being and that is God. If you want to give, first you have to receive from someone who has already in infinite measure. If you do not receive, how are you going to give? How is it possible?

Self-criticism is not the way
That leads to self-perfection;
Neither is self-flattery.
Through conscious self-awareness alone,
The seeker reaches his goal.

One does not have to abandon the outer life in order to make spiritual progress. One has only to go deep within. Then one has to see how much of the outer life is really necessary in order to lead a spiritual life and achieve God-realisation.

There are many silly, useless things which we do in the ordinary life, which we have to discard. Again, there are many things in the outer life which we call duty, soulful duty. But when we enter into the deepest spiritual life, at that time we have no duty. Before we reach that stage, we have to fulfil some earthly duties. But when it is a matter of choosing between the outer and inner life, we have to pay more attention to the inner life. Then we will have solid joy, peace, love and power. Then whatever is unnecessary in the outer life we can transform. But there are things that are of paramount importance in the outer life which we must accept. Things which have to be given up in the outer life we shall give up. We have to simplify our life. God is very simple; we are complex. Inside simplicity is purity; inside purity is divinity.

My Lord,
This is my sincere prayer:
Please do not fulfil my desires.
Only manifest Yourself
In and through me.
I do not want anything from You
Except whatever You want to give.

I meditate on God not because God will give me everything I want. I meditate on God because God will give me only the things that I need.

A true spiritual seeker feels that there is a link between the inner world and the outer world. And something else he also feels. He feels that if we feed the inner world, then only can the outer world have its true meaning. The body is the outer world. Daily we feed the body three times without fail. We have been doing it and we shall keep on doing it until we breathe our last. But again, there is deep within us a divine child called the soul. To keep the body alive we eat, but to help the soul, to fulfil its divine mission on earth, we have no time. Unless and until the soul, which is the conscious representative of God in us, is fulfilled, we can never be fulfilled in our outer life.

If you do not keep
Your God-appointment
Early in the morning,
Then during the entire day
You will be blessed with
Bitter disappointment.

Do not try to approach God with your thinking mind. It may only stimulate your intellectual ideas, activities and beliefs. Try to approach God with your crying heart. It will awaken your soulful, spiritual consciousness.

If we know the divine art of concentration, if we know the divine art of meditation, if we know the divine art of contemplation, easily and consciously we can unite the inner world and the outer world. And to our widest surprise we shall see that the outer world, which is now full of complexity, disharmony and so forth, is bound to become harmonious, simple, straight-forward and genuine. The inner life has the capacity to simplify the complexities of the outer life. The inner world and the outer world must go together. Otherwise, what will happen? The inner life will have to wait for millennia to offer God's Truth to the world at large and the outer life will remain a barren desert for millennia.

Each soulful prayer
And each heartful meditation
Can and will, without fail,
Create a confidence-giant
In the God-seeker's life.

People have many dreams, but I have only three: perfect peace between the soul and body, the total transformation of my nature and complete satisfaction in God's entire creation.

There is definitely a link between the inner and the outer worlds. We have to consciously feel this link, and finally we have to touch and strengthen the link with our soul's determination and body's dedicated service and willingness. Now the body listens to the mind. When the mind says, "Go this way," the body goes. The next moment the mind says, "No, no, no! That is the wrong way to go. Follow some other direction," and the body follows. In this way the body is caught by limitations. But far beyond the domain of the mind is the soul. The soul is flooded with light. If we consciously try to have a free access to the inner being, to the soul, then naturally the light of the soul will come to the fore and it will help us at every moment to deal with the tenebrous darkness in us and around us. Finally, we will see that either we have transformed darkness into light or we have come millions and millions of miles away from darkness and are bathing in the sea of infinite light.

The wish of my soul:
My body will become
A perfect instrument of God.
The wish of my body:
My soul will be
My body's ever-leading
And ever-forgiving captain.

For a genuine truth-seeker the outer life and the inner life are one, and that life has only one message: God comes first, spirituality comes first.

If the physical body listens to the soul and not to the doubtful, doubting and sophisticated, complex, destructive, unaspiring mind, at every moment the link between the inner world and the outer world will be strengthened and one will complete the other. That is to say, the inner world will need the outer world as its chariot and the outer world will need the inner world as its charioteer. If there is a chariot without a charioteer, it is useless, for without a charioteer the chariot cannot move. Again, if there is a charioteer without a chariot, he is also useless. So both the charioteer and the chariot are necessary. They are of equal importance. Similarly, the outer life and the inner life are of equal importance.

The outer life is the body,
The inner life is the heart.
What can one do without the other?
Wherever one goes,
The other has to follow.

He who has accepted spirituality in the truest sense of the term has first to feel that God is the sole reality. Then he will see that God's creation can never be separated from God.

A spiritual aspirant who is crying for God, who is constantly shedding soulful tears, trying to become one with God, feels that God is in the inmost recesses of his heart. He has not to go to the Himalayan caves in order to realise God. His God lives inside him. He feels that because God is inside him, God's creation is also inside him. A spiritual person always feels that God's entire creation is his home.

My heart knows
That perfect perfection can abide
Only in my life's conscious
God-reflection.

Service is self-expansion. A sincere seeker serves precisely because he knows that there is and there can be nothing other than service. When he serves aspiring humanity, it is because his inner necessity commands him to serve.

Service is very often misunderstood. We feel that if we are going to serve, we have to serve each and every one, all and sundry. But in the spiritual life, we know that service has to be rendered only to those who are ready to receive it. If not, our service will be misunderstood. If somebody is fast asleep and you try to arouse that person because you see that the sun is up, he may become angry or displeased. He may say, "What right do you have to disturb my precious sleep?" Only if our service is rendered to someone who wants to be awakened or who is ready to be awakened, to someone who wants light or who needs light, can our service be properly used.

Love God
To please yourself.
Serve God
To please Him.

Your soulful patience is the first rung on your fruitful peace-ladder.

The world is still millions of miles away from world-peace. But just because we do not see the reality all at once, that is no reason to become discouraged. Before the day dawns, it is dark. When we look at the darkness that is all around and identify with the darkness, it is almost impossible for us to have faith that there will be light. But at the end of the tunnel there is light. At the end of the darkness there is light.

Since yours is a calm and serene mind,
Your hope of promoting world-peace
Shall not remain an unfulfilled dream.

When the age of reason ends, the heart of peace will inundate the entire world.

Right now the countries of the world misunderstand each other, and some of them are undivine, to say the least. But deep within them there is an inner urge. Each nation hopes to someday have peace, light and oneness. Peace, light and oneness will definitely come into the world-arena precisely because each nation is inundated with hope. This hope of today will be transformed into the abiding satisfaction of tomorrow only when we believe in hope, grow into hope, and breathe in at every moment the fragrance and the beauty of hope.

*Indeed, the choice
Of humanity's divinity is perfect.
It desires to see
All seekers living together
As good members
Of a single world-community.*

Action can be done without asking God's Wisdom, but if we beg of God's Wisdom to guide us and then we act, then it is God's responsibility.

To start my spiritual journey, I need God the Forgiveness. First I have to empty myself of my undivine existence. All the undivine thoughts and undivine deeds that are inside me, everything that is unaspiring and uninspiring within me, I have to discard. And for that I need God's Forgiveness. I have committed Himalayan blunders countless times. If God does not forgive me for the undivine things that I have done over the years, then how can I walk along the spiritual path, the sunlit path? Only if God forgives me can I enter wholeheartedly into the spiritual life. So, to start with, I need God's Forgiveness.

My Lord Beloved Supreme,
I am my desire-desert.
Can You not be Your Forgiveness-River?

Every seeker has to give to the Supreme what is best in him.

At every moment I am assailed by bad thoughts or inspired by good thoughts. When I am assailed by a bad thought, I will try to discard it. When I am inspired by a good thought, I will try to develop and enlarge it. When I start meditating early in the morning, if one good thought comes, I will try to enlarge it. Let us say it is a thought of divine love—not human, emotional love, but divine, universal love—"I love God, I love God's entire creation." This thought can be expanded. I can think of love as my ideal, as my ultimate Goal. In this way, if I think of divine love, universal love, transcendental love, then I am identifying myself with the Goal itself.

Ask your mind to be
A child of illumination
And not
A merchant of confusion.

MAY

Be kind, be all sympathy,
For each and every human being
Is forced to fight against himself.

~ MAY 1 ~

God's Compassion exists in every life-experience of yours, whether you believe it or not.

When I feel that God, out of His infinite Bounty, has forgiven me, at that time I can think of another aspect of God, and that is God's Compassion. God has forgiven me; now I need His Compassion. I need His Compassion because I am weak, I am ignorant and I am in every way a failure. I fervently desire to do something, to achieve something, to become something, but I do not have the capacity to do what I want to do or to grow into what I want to become. Therefore, I desperately need God's Compassion. Without God's Compassion I will not be able to achieve anything, and I will not be able to become anything.

Do not depend on
Earthly applause.
Depend only on
God's Compassion-Smile.

Powerless is human help. Therefore, look above for help.

After receiving God's Forgiveness and Compassion, I need God's Blessings. I need God to shower His infinite Blessings on me from above, so that I can succeed in the battlefield of life. Life is a constant battle, and if I am to succeed, then I have to entirely depend on God's Blessings. If He blesses my devoted head and surrendered heart, only then can I succeed in life and proceed along the spiritual path.

With God's Grace
We begin.
With God's Encouragement
We continue.

Whether you accept or reject it, God's Love for you is permanent.

After God has forgiven me, granted me His Compassion and showered His Blessings upon me, then I have to feel at every moment God's Love. I have to feel that the One who has forgiven me, shown me His Compassion and blessed me, really cares for me. If I feel that God really loves me, then only can I have true and abiding happiness. The Creator is all love for His creation. But the creation quite often does not feel it or realise it. Since I am part of God's creation, it is my bounden duty to feel God's Love at every moment. Only then will I try to become good, divine and perfect, and please Him in His own way.

A God-lover's best attitude:
God cared for me,
God cares for me
And God will always care for me.

To see beyond myself is to find and feel my inseparable oneness with my Beloved Supreme.

After God's Love, something very significant and very deep I have to feel, and that is God's Oneness. God's Love is not enough. I can love someone or something, but I may not have established my oneness, inseparable oneness, with that person or that thing. So after I have felt God's Love, I have to develop my conscious, constant and inseparable oneness with Him.

Awareness is the only thing
That my mind needs.
Soulfulness is the only thing
That my heart needs.
Oneness—my constant, sleepless,
Inseparable oneness with my Lord Supreme—
Is the only thing that I need.

Perfection means constant rejection of your desire-life. Perfection means constant acceptance of your aspiration-heart.

In order to have conscious, constant and inseparable oneness with God, I have to achieve something and become something, and that thing is perfection. How do I become perfect? I become perfect by crying inwardly to receive the things that will uplift me and illumine me, and to conquer the things that torment me and disturb me. When I cry to receive good things and to conquer bad things, God is pleased with me. It is only by pleasing God that I can become perfect.

Every day I tell my Beloved Supreme
That I can be absolutely perfect.
Every day my Beloved Supreme tells me
That I am His chosen child.

To obey God's Will is to escape from one's self-created prison.

When my heart's only cry is to please God in His own way, then God can manifest Himself in and through me. When my inner cry carries me to God, I say to Him, "O my Beloved Supreme, make me Your perfect instrument." When God comes to me, He gives me a broad Smile—a wide, soulful, illumining Smile—and says, "My child, I shall make you My perfect instrument and, at the same time, I will manifest Myself in and through you."

With physical courage
We take pride
In breaking the world
In our own way.
With the courage of the spirit
We offer the world to God.
We place the world, our world,
At the Feet of God
So that He may guide and mould
The world, our world,
In His own way.

Your inner life is crumbling. You will have to start all over again. Rest assured, this is not an uncommon experience in human life.

Let us take discipline as a muscle. Overnight you cannot develop most powerful muscles. Slowly and steadily you have to develop them. First you have to know how many minutes you can meditate. If you can meditate for five minutes, this means that for these five minutes you are disciplining yourself. Early in the morning, while your friends and dear ones are still in the world of sleep, if you get up to pray and meditate for five minutes, you are disciplining yourself.

You must love
Your daily discipline-life.
Then only will God grant you
The key to His Heart's Fulness-Door.

A life of indulgence will, without fail, have sad side-effects.

How can you increase your discipline? The easiest way is to develop a true thirst, an inner cry, for the fruits of discipline. You can do this by seeing what happens when you lead a disciplined life and when you do not lead a disciplined life. You yourself have to be the judge. When you get up at five or six o'clock and meditate for fifteen minutes or half an hour, you feel extremely good. You feel that the whole world is beautiful. You love everybody and everybody loves you. God's creation is all love for you, and you are all love for God's creation. Because you got up and meditated, you are inundated with good thoughts.

Love your goal!
Automatically
You will make progress.

If we do not breathe in life-energy, we cannot live. Similarly, without peace we do not and cannot live like true human beings.

We desperately need peace—peace within, peace without. So how is it that we do not have peace, which is so important in our life? We do not have peace because of our hunger for possession. We want to possess the world, but when we increase our material possessions, we come to realise that we are still veritable beggars. No matter what we acquire in our life, when we look around we see that somebody else has that very thing in greater measure, and we lose our peace of mind. We become victims to worry, anxiety, depression and frustration, which is always followed by destruction.

O seeker,
The joy of your desire-life
Is nothing but your sorrow
Masked.

Desires are truly fulfilled only when they are perfectly transcended.

Possession brings frustration, and renunciation is fruitless. What then, can give us peace of mind? Only acceptance of God's Will can give us true peace of mind. By accepting God's Will as our own, very own, we can get peace. Then only can our life be fruitful. In God's Eye there is no such thing as possession and renunciation. In God's Eye there is only one thing: acceptance—acceptance of God's Will. In our heart, in our life, there is only one ultimate prayer, the prayer that the Saviour Christ has taught us: "Let Thy Will be done." Millions of prayers have been written from time immemorial, but no prayer can equal this one: "Let Thy Will be done." When we accept God's Will as our own, at every moment peace looms large in our life of wisdom, in our life of aspiration and in our life of dedication.

To master life's teeming problems,
Come out of the snare of teeming desires
And try to befriend the perfection-will
Of Infinity's satisfaction-heart.

Pray so that you can tell God what you have been doing. Meditate so that God can effectively tell you what you are supposed to do.

How can we know if something is God's Will? When something is God's Will, we will feel a kind of inner joy or satisfaction even before we start doing it. While working, we will also get joy. Finally, we feel that we will be equally happy if our action is fruitful or fruitless. In the ordinary life we are happy only when success dawns. Only when we see victory at the end of our journey are we happy and delighted. But if we can have the same kind of happiness, joy and satisfaction whether we succeed or fail, and if we can cheerfully offer the result of our actions at the Feet of our Beloved Supreme, then only can we know that what we have done is God's Will. Otherwise, when there is success, we feel that what we did was God's Will, and when there is failure, we say that what we did was the will of a hostile force. Or when we succeed we say it is because of our personal effort, our will, and when we fail we say it is because God does not care for us.

Only when we please God
In God's own way
Shall we feel comfort.
Otherwise,
Everything will be an ordeal.

Whatever takes place in the divine Providence is not only for the best, but also inevitable, because there is no alternative.

Success and failure are two experiences. These two experiences we have to unify, and whichever experience we get at the end of our endeavour, we have to offer to the Supreme with tremendous joy. If we can place the result at the Feet of our Beloved Supreme soulfully, cheerfully, unreservedly and unconditionally, then without fail we will have true peace of mind. At that time peace of mind will come and knock at our life's door. We will not have to wait for peace of mind; it will be waiting for us.

Perfect happiness is
Enthusiasm minus
Expectation.

Our vital loves to be loved. Our heart loves so that it can also be loved. Our soul just loves devotedly and eternally.

You can be more receptive to divine love if you can feel every day that your Source is all Love, and that you are on earth to offer constantly, in thought and in action, the love that you already have. At every moment you have many thoughts, so you can offer love through each of your thoughts. And each time you do something, you can feel that this action is nothing but an expression of love. While thinking and while acting, if you can feel that you are offering love to mankind, to the rest of the world, then you can be more receptive to the universal love. In this way you can feel that God's divine Love is all for you.

It is God the Lover inside you
Who offers the world joy and love.
It is God the Beloved who receives it
In the world-heart.

Humility is not a self-imposed, willed virtue. It is an inner state of consciousness that feels pure joy in its expression.

There is a great difference between humility and unworthiness. When we are about to do something, certain incapacities that we are born with may make us feel unworthy. Again, unworthiness may come as a result of something undivine that we have done. But whatever the reason, he who feels unworthy of something will automatically remain far away from the world of delight. This is a negative way of approaching the truth. But if we take the positive approach, then we feel always that we have come from God. We have to be conscious of God within us, not through the feeling of unworthiness, but through humility. If I am unworthy of my Source, then why did the Source create me?

Try to see yourself
From now on
The way God has always
Been seeing you:
As His universal Vision-fulfiller.

We must realise that there is only one way of acquiring infinite future possibilities. That way lies in the great power: humility.

By feeling unworthy we will not be able to draw God's Compassion. It is absurd. Not even one drop more of God's Compassion will rain down on earth if we feel that we are unworthy. Far from it. But if we are humble, if we aspire and feel that the little capacity that we have has come from God, then we can fulfil ourselves and God will be pleased. So never feel unworthy. Only feel the necessity of real humility in your life so that God can act in and through you on your own level.

My humility-life
Is my conscious oneness
With the illumining and fulfilling Universality
Of my Beloved Supreme.

We shall never hear the song of the inner voice if we consciously or unconsciously make friends with anxiety.

When we are assailed by worries and anxieties, we have to feel that there is an antidote. The antidote is to feel inwardly God's Love for us. Worries and anxieties will go away only when we identify ourselves with something that has peace, poise, divinity and the feeling of absolute oneness. If we identify ourselves with the Inner Pilot, then we get the strength of His illumining Light. Worries come because we identify ourselves with fear. By worrying all the time or by thinking undivine thoughts, we will never move towards our goal. We will enter into divinity only by having positive thoughts: "I am of God. I am for God." If we think this, then there can be no worry, no anxiety.

Devour your anxieties!
God's Happiness and your happiness
Will fly together in oneness-sky.

No doubt, man is infinitely superior to a wild beast. But he always drinks two bottles of poison: one bottle is ego and the other is doubt. Until he has done away with these two bottles, man is no more than a higher animal.

Doubt is an undivine force. I call it a slow poison. Doubt is our worst enemy in the spiritual life. Today I doubt myself, tomorrow I doubt God, the day after tomorrow I doubt the whole world. If I doubt God, nothing happens; God remains as perfect as ever. If I doubt some other individual, that person remains the same. But when I doubt myself, I am ruined. I can not go even one inch forward. So the best thing is not to doubt oneself, not to doubt others and not to doubt God.

Why do you allow doubt
To spoil the perfection
Of your mind?
Why do you allow fear
To spoil the perfection
Of your heart?
Why do you allow anxiety
To spoil the perfection
Of your life?

A doubting mind is a shameless threat to your heart's cherished tranquility.

The best and most effective way to conquer doubt is to take the positive side. Feel that you are not doubt; you are certainty. Feel that you are not fear; you are courage. Always try to identify yourself with the positive quality. If you change your inner attitude towards your own inner life, then you will say that doubt is not reality, fear is not reality; the real reality is faith, the real reality is courage.

Do not allow yourself
To be trampled constantly
By the feet of doubt and fear!

Our Goal is within us. To reach that Goal we have to take to the spiritual life.

In the spiritual life, the thing that is most needed is awareness or consciousness. Without this, everything is a barren desert. When we enter into a dark place, we take a flashlight or some other light in order to know where we are going. If we want to know about our unlit life, we have to take the help of consciousness. We know that the sun illumines the world. But how are we aware of it? We are aware of it through our consciousness, which is self-revealing. The functioning of the sun is not self-revealing. It is our consciousness of the sun that makes us feel that the sun illumines the world. It is our consciousness that is self-revealing in everything. And this consciousness is an infinite sea of delight.

Be brave
Where your heart is concerned.
Be sincere
Where your mind is concerned.
Then you will see how easy it is
To live your life
In a supremely better consciousness.

Faith has been chosen by God Himself to be the campaign manager for God's Victory.

Having faith in God and having faith in oneself is the perfect answer to all questions. But our faith has to be something inner and deep within. It is not mere outer vital confidence in oneself. This faith is the river that is flowing into the sea of ever-growing, ever-illumining reality.

By defying doubt,
His mind is flying
In the sky of God's
Satisfaction-Delight.

To see the Beyond, what is absolutely necessary is our certainty—our implicit faith in ourselves. We have to feel that we are God's chosen child.

In order to realise the Goal deep within, we have to renew our life and make it fresh every day. Each day early in the morning we have to revitalise our outer life with golden hope. This hope is not an idle dream; it is the precursor of the divinity which will manifest in and through our outer nature. It is our dynamic divine quality, our golden hope, that sees the Beyond even when it is still a far cry.

O heart, my heart,
I have only one prayer.
Do become the banner of hope
In my life.

Allow others to enjoy their superficial superiority. You try to enjoy the purity of your heart's satisfaction-unity.

Sometimes, in order to prove his superiority, man tries to exercise his power violently, aggressively. He wants to derive joy from his superiority. He wants to prove to the world that he is important. In order to prove his eminence he adopts any means, and his conscience does not bother him. God, out of His infinite Bounty, comes to him and says, "This is a wrong choice. You cannot prove to the world that you are matchless, unique. What you actually crave from your superiority is joy, boundless joy. But this boundless joy will never be yours unless you know the secret of secrets. And that secret is your indivisible oneness with each human being on earth."

Your strong reliance
Upon your own capacities
Will be the downfall
Of your spiritual life.

Happy is he who has overcome all selfishness. Blessed is he who sees God emerging from the sea of ego.

The ordinary human ego gives us a sense of separate identity, separate consciousness. No doubt, a sense of individuality and self-importance is necessary at a certain stage in man's development. But the ego separates our individual consciousness from the Universal Consciousness. The very function of the ego is separation. It cannot feel satisfaction in viewing two things at a time on the same level. It always feels that one must be superior to the other. So the ego makes us feel that we are all separate weaklings, that it will never be possible for us to be or to have the infinite Consciousness. The ego, finally, is limitation. This limitation is ignorance, and ignorance is death. So ego ultimately ends in death.

Like other things,
Discard your list
Of grievances.
Discard your self-styled
Importance.

There is one defeat that brings us a greater triumph than even victory does. What is that defeat? The defeat of our ego by our soul.

We weaken the ego and ultimately subdue it by thinking of God's all-pervading Consciousness. This consciousness is not something that we have to achieve. This consciousness is already within us; we just have to be aware of it. Further, while we are in meditation we have to develop it and illumine it to infinite proportions. And to our wide surprise, the ego will be buried in the bosom of death.

O Lord,
Do give me the capacity
To love Your Silence-Sound
Infinitely more than I love
Anything else.

Wait for tomorrow to think tomorrow's thoughts.

From the spiritual point of view, each thought carries a special weight in our mind. Each thought has a special significance. In our ordinary life we all know what a thought is. We create thought. We cherish thought. There is nobody who does not know how to think—ordinary thinking, that is. But if one who has a developed mind stops thinking, if he has learned the art of stopping the mind, he makes tremendous progress in the spiritual life. When a thought enters into the aspiring mind, it is like meeting an enemy in the battlefield. The more one can silence the mind, the sooner one realises the Goal.

God loves you
When He sees your heart
Flooded with silence.
God loves you
When He sees your mind
Empty of its usual contents:
Confusion-forest.

Are you casting about for true happiness in life? If so, yield not to reason, yield not to fate, but yield only to the dictates of your inner voice.

God's Will in an individual is progressive, like a muscle developing—strong, stronger, strongest. God's Will is to make an individual feel that there is something abiding, lasting, everlasting. When an individual reaches that stage, he will know God's ultimate Will. God's Will we can know from the sense of abiding satisfaction it gives us. Anything that is eternal, anything that is immortal, anything that is divine, is God's Will. Even though God deals with Eternity, He is not indifferent even for one second. For it is from one second, two seconds, three seconds that we enter into Infinity and Eternity. Let us try to feel what God's Will is at every second.

God does not want
To fulfil your desire
Precisely because
He wants to fulfil His own desire.
What is God's desire?
His desire is to make you
Exactly like Him: another God.

The more we inwardly obey, the better we outwardly rule.

There is a very simple way to know what God's Will is for us as individuals. Every day when we start our day we build our own world. We make decisions. We feel that things have to be done in a certain way. I have to deal with this person in this way. I have to say this; I have to do this; I have to give this. Everything is I, I, I. If, instead of planning, we can make our minds absolutely calm and silent, we can know God's Will. This silence is not the silence of a dead body; it is the dynamic, progressive silence of receptivity.

A true God-lover
Does not have to abide
By his mind's decisions.
He has only to listen
To his heart's dictates.

Through total silence and the ever-increasing receptivity of the mind, God's Will can be known.

When the human mind works powerfully, the divine Will cannot work. God's Will works only when the human mind does not work. When the mind becomes a pure vessel, the Supreme can pour into it His infinite Peace, Light and Bliss. So the easiest way for us to know God's Will is to become the instrument and not the doer. If we become only the instrument for carrying out God's Plans, God's Will will act in and through us. God does the acting and He is the action. He is everything. We only observe.

When your aspiration-dedication-life
Is on earth
Only for the fulfilment of God's Will,
Then you are bound to feel
That your success-life
And progress-heart
Are nothing other than
An effortless effort.

Love mankind here, soulfully and sleep-lessly. The reward you will get elsewhere, unmistakably plus infinitely.

You can consciously give pure love to others if you feel that you are giving a portion of your life-breath when you talk to others or think of others. And this life-breath you are offering just because you feel that you and the rest of the world are totally and inseparably one. Where there is one-ness, it is all pure love.

Each time I love mankind
Unreservedly,
Each time I love God
Unconditionally,
I reclaim a part
Of my own real life.

A life of purity is a life of self-sufficiency, because it is deeply rooted in love divine.

Love is the source of humanity, love is the source of divinity. Human love ultimately ends in frustration. Why? Because human love proceeds from one limited body-consciousness to another limited body-consciousness. Divine love is all illumination. At the journey's start, in the middle of the race and at the journey's close it is all illumination. Divine love descends from the soul-freedom into the body-consciousness. Divine love is the sun of freedom both in Heaven and on earth.

The fragrance of a pure heart
Always intensifies
Your life's satisfaction-delight.

Man can be happy and safe only when the heart feels faster than the mind thinks.

Each problem is a force. When we see the problem, we feel deep within us a greater force. And when we face the problem we prove to the problem that we not only have the greatest force, but we are the greatest force on earth. A problem increases when the heart hesitates and the mind calculates. A problem decreases when the heart braves the problem and the mind supports the heart. A problem diminishes when the mind uses its search-light and the heart uses its illumination-light.

> *When outer difficulties*
> *Stand in front of you,*
> *Just tell yourself,*
> *"If I can meditate*
> *In spite of this opposition,*
> *I will become*
> *A better and stronger God-seeker*
> *And God-lover."*

JUNE

Surrender, cheerfully surrender
To God's Will.
You will not be buffeted
By the strong winds of worry.

Self-denial cannot solve any problem. Self-assertion cannot solve any problem. It is God-manifestation through self-existence that can solve all problems of the present and the future.

If fear is our problem, then we have to feel that we are the chosen soldiers of God the Almighty. If doubt is our problem, then we have to feel that we have deep within us the sea of God's Light. If jealousy is our problem, we have to feel that we are the oneness of God's Light and Truth. If insecurity is our problem, then we have to feel that God is nothing and can be nothing other than constant and ceaseless assurance to us that He will claim us as His very own. If the body is the problem, our constant alertness and attention can solve this problem. If the vital is the problem, our soaring imagination can solve this problem. If the mind is the problem, our illumining inspiration can solve this problem. If the heart is the problem, our perfecting aspiration can solve this problem. If life is the problem, our fulfilling self-discovery can solve this problem.

Only a God-focused mind
Can challenge all doubt-storms
And all jealousy-trains.

We agonise ourselves in trying to make a problem vanish. God laughs at us. But as soon as we accept a difficulty as inevitable, ordained by Him, it slowly melts away until the day comes when we wonder where it has disappeared.

If we know how to look at a problem, half the strength of the problem goes away. But usually we try to avoid the problem; we try to run away from it. A problem is not an indication of any fault or crime of ours, so why should we be afraid to face it? We must know that there are also wrong forces, undivine forces, hostile forces around us. By blaming ourselves and then trying to hide, we do not solve the problem. We have to face the problem and see whether we really are to blame. We have to feel that we are not the problem-maker but the problem-solver. We have to practise the spiritual life and develop inner strength, aspiration and inner detachment. Slowly, gradually, we will become inwardly strong, and then we will be able to solve the problems caused by our own inner weaknesses.

The darkness within you
Will die
Only when the devotedness within you
Invokes illumination from above.

Human life is at once a burden and a blessing. It compels man to bear continual suffering. It gives man also a great promise of God-realisation.

Prosperity and adversity are the two eyes that we all have. Adversity leads us inward to correct and perfect our march of life. Prosperity leads us outward to illumine and immortalise our human birth. In prosperity our inner strength remains static. In adversity our inner strength becomes dynamic. None can deny the fact that every step of progress which the world has made has come from both the smiles of prosperity and the tears of adversity. Adversity, like poverty, is no sin. One merit of adversity none can deny: it helps us to be stronger within. The stronger we are within, the brighter we are without. One who is afraid of studying in the school of adversity can never hope for a perfect education in life. How often is our aspiration forced into play by dire adversity; but in glorious prosperity how rarely it peeps out.

Obstacles are meant
To be surmounted.
Shun self-doubts
And be victorious.

The doubting mind is nothing other than an insecurity-plant.

Faith and doubt. These are like the North and the South Pole. Unfortunately, a man of faith is very often misunderstood. We are apt to call a man of faith a fanatic. Here we make a deplorable mistake. A fanatic hates reason and ignores the reasoning mind; whereas a man of faith, if he is really a man of faith, will welcome reason and accept the doubting mind. Then his faith will help the doubting mind to transcend itself into the infinite Vast, into something eternal and immortal.

Be wise!
Constantly keep
Your inner fears and doubts
Under your perfect control.

To face failure and greet success, one must deliberately go out of the doubt-territory.

We doubt God precisely because we think He is invisible. We doubt Him because we think He is inaudible. We doubt Him because we think He is incomprehensible. But to see Him, what have we done? To hear Him, what have we done? To understand Him, what have we done? To see Him, have we prayed soulfully every day? The answer is no. To hear Him, have we loved mankind devotedly? No. To understand Him, have we served the divinity in humanity? No. We have not prayed to God. We have not loved mankind. We have not served the divinity in humanity. Yet we want to see God face to face. It is impossible.

What has caused your failures?
Not your doubt,
Not your insecurity,
But your unwillingness.

You are lost when you believe your doubts.
You are dead when you doubt your beliefs.

Doubt can be conquered. It has to be conquered. How? The only answer is constant and soulful concentration on the mind, meditation on the heart and contemplation on the entire being. How to conquer doubt? Observe the vow of inner silence; do inner meditation and selfless service. Your doubt will have no strength to shout at you. It has to die and it will, for good.

If you want to be a devoted member
Of God's society,
Then immediately reject what you are not:
Venom-doubt,
And soulfully accept what you are:
God's choice instrument.

Self-pity, self-indulgence and egoistic emotional cries are but one shortcoming with different names.

If you say that you have no faith in yourself but you have all faith in God, then I wish to say you cannot go very far. You have to have faith, constant faith and abundant faith, not only in God, but also in yourself since you are God's son or God's daughter. When you truly feel that you are God's child, you will find that it is beneath your dignity to make friends with ignorance. Reality, Eternity, Immortality and Infinity are not vague terms; these are your birthright. When you have that kind of faith, God will shower His choicest blessings upon your devoted head and surrendered heart.

You cannot transcend yourself
By book studies.
But you can definitely transcend yourself
By paying attention
To the inner dictates of your soul.

**Meditation is the expansion of conscious-
ness. When you are meditating, if you feel
and know that along with you someone else
will benefit from your meditation, then this
is absolutely perfect meditation.**

We who have started walking along the spiritual
path are the forerunners. All will eventually run
toward the same transcendental Goal. The major-
ity of mankind will not always lag behind. All children of God, no matter how unconscious and
unaspiring, will one day run toward the common
Goal. This Goal is the supreme discovery of one's
divinity and the constant and perfect manifestation of one's everlasting reality.

*You are trying to liberate the world.
Before you can do that,
You have to raise
Your own spiritual standard
High, very high.*

What is spirituality? It is the common language of man and God.

When we follow the spiritual life, when we walk along the path of spirituality, one word constantly looms large, and that word is sacrifice. We have to sacrifice our very existence for others—what we have and what we are. What we have is willingness and what we are is cheerfulness. This cheerfulness we can have only when we go deep within. When we are cheerfulness within, we are willingness without. If our inner existence is flooded with joy and delight, then only shall we be eager, more than eager, to help the outer world.

When I cheerfully do
What I can,
My Lord Supreme unconditionally
Does for me
What I cannot.

It is such a difficult task to gain peace of mind. Why do you then spend your mind's peace so extravagantly?

How to conquer anger? Feel the necessity of perfecting yourself. When anger wants to enter into you, say, "I am so sorry. I eat only one food. The name of my food is peace. I will not be able to digest you. If ever I eat you, I will be destroyed within and without. I do not want to be destroyed. I have to do much for the divinity in me and the humanity around me. O anger, you are knocking at the wrong door."

Because he contained his anger,
The divine forces had the opportunity
To act in and through him
And finally to illumine him.

You may suppress something for some time, but you cannot avoid it forever. Therefore, suppression of anything is not and cannot be the answer. The illumination of that very thing is imperative.

In our daily life we do not have to suppress emotion. We do not have to suppress anything. Suppression is very bad. If we suppress something today, tomorrow we will be subjected to its revolt. Suppression is not the answer. What we have to do is to illumine our emotion. While we are illumining it, we shall feel real joy. By suppressing, what do we actually accomplish? Nothing. We are only forcing ourselves beyond our capacity and sincere willingness. As we have a desire to enjoy a life of pleasure, so also we have a desire to suppress life. A life of pleasure and a life of suppression are equally bad. Both are followed by frustration and frustration ends in destruction.

Life has given you
What you unconsciously wanted to have:
Frustration.
You can consciously get from life
What you need to have:
Illumination.

What is patience? It is an inner assurance of God's unreserved love and unconditional guidance.

Patience is a divine virtue. Unfortunately, not only are we badly wanting in this divine virtue, but we also neglect it most foolishly. Patience is God's power hidden in us to weather the teeming storms of life. If failure has the strength to turn your life into bitterness itself, then patience has the strength to turn your life into the sweetest joy. Do not surrender to fate after a single failure. Failure, at most, precedes success. But success once achieved, confidence becomes your name.

Do not be afraid of tasting
The bitterness of failure.
Be brave!
The sweetness of success
Will before long befriend you.

Patience is not something passive. On the contrary, it is something dynamic.

How to develop patience? In order to develop patience, we have to feel that we have launched into a spiritual journey, an inner journey, which has a Goal, and that this Goal wants us and needs us as much as we want and need it. This Goal is ready to accept us, to give us what it has, but it will do this in its own way at the choice Hour of God. We must know that God will give us His wealth in time. Patience will never tell us that it is a hopeless task. Patience will only tell us either that we are not ready or that the time is not ripe.

He who wants to be
A God-lover and God-server
Can never be satisfied
With a limited supply of patience.

Do not visit the worlds of ego-exhibition if you want to keep your own ego under perfect control.

My human pride feels that I can do everything. My divine pride, the pride that has surrendered itself to the Will of God, knows that I can do everything only when I am inspired, guided and helped by the Supreme. My human pride wants the world to understand me, my love, my help and sacrifice. My divine pride, which is the feeling of oneness with all in God, does not wish the world to understand my selfless activities. It feels that if God understands me, knows my motives, then there can be no greater reward.

If you are prompted
To measure your service-life,
Then your entire being
Cannot reach out
Toward God-Perfection.

I love my heart's tiny humility-nest infinitely more than my mind's huge arrogance-palace.

My humility does not mean that I want the world to ignore me. That is no humility. My humility says that I should neither veil my ignorance nor make a parade of my knowledge. To be violently dissatisfied with oneself and curse one's fate is not the sign of humility. The true signs of humility are one's constant aspiration and one's inner cry for more peace, light and bliss.

When God reaches down
To touch the finite,
We call it Compassion.
When man bows down
In self-offering to humanity,
We call it humility.

If you go on your selfless way slowly and steadily, God will soon quietly lead you.

God is my superior, my only superior. I am humble to Him. This is my supreme duty. God's children are my equals. I am humble to them. This is my greatest necessity. Pride is my inferior. I am humble to pride. This is my surest safety. My humility is not the abstinence from self-love. I love myself. I really do. I love myself because in me the highest divinity proudly breathes.

It is an exceptional privilege
To have the beauty of a serene mind,
The purity of a loving heart
And
The divinity of a humble life.

A soulful heart has discovered a supreme truth: to meditate on God is a privilege and not a duty.

When we meditate in the heart, we come to realise that God is infinite and God is omnipotent. If He is infinite, on the strength of His omnipotence He can also be finite. He exists in our multifarious activities; He is everywhere. He includes everything; He excludes nothing. This is what our inner meditation can tell us. Our heart's meditation also tells us that God is dearer than the dearest and that He is our only Beloved.

Why does the heart want to meditate?
The heart wants to meditate
Because it wants to love
The Supreme more.
The heart knows that meditation
Is the answer.

Cultivate purity in your heart. Before long you will be able to rediscover the Kingdom of Heaven.

The inner light is purity. The outer life is ignorance. The inner light wants to conquer the outer ignorance. Likewise, the outer ignorance wants to conquer and devour the inner light. The inner light wants to conquer the outer ignorance with a view to transforming it. When the outer ignorance is transformed, it becomes a divine warrior fighting to establish the Kingdom of Heaven here on earth.

If you are a true God-lover
Then you will see
That God has created everything
For your pure heart
And not for your critical eyes.

When you see that a person's defects and bad qualities are obvious, try to feel immediately that his defects and bad qualities do not represent him totally. His real self is infinitely better than what you see now.

If humanity had to become perfect before it could be accepted by you, then it would not need your love, affection and concern. But right now, in its imperfect state of consciousness, humanity does need your help. Give humanity unreservedly even the most insignificant and limited help that you have at your disposal. This is the golden opportunity. Once you miss this opportunity, your future suffering will be beyond your endurance, because a day will come when you will realise that humanity's imperfection is your own imperfection. You are God's creation; so is humanity. Humanity is only an expression of your universal heart. You can and must love humanity, not just as a whole, but also specifically, if you realise the fact that until humanity has realised its supreme Goal, your own divine perfection will not be complete.

Your daily life is peopled with
Seekers and non-seekers,
God-doubters and God-believers.
Your eye of concern
Encompasses them
And your heart of love
Teaches them.

The only effective way to love man is to first love God sleeplessly.

The end of all inner teaching is love: divine love, not human love. Human love binds; the result is frustration. And at the end of frustration, destruction looms large. But divine love is expansion, enlargement, the feeling of true oneness. So if we love someone, we have to know that we love him precisely because deep inside that person is God. It is not because the person is my father, or my mother, or my sister, or my brother, that I love him. No. I love him just because inside him I feel, I see the living presence of my dearest Beloved.

Because I fear God,
I do not have to fear any man.
Because I love God,
I have to love all human beings.

Your mind thinks nothing is worth believing. Your heart feels nobody is worth loving. No wonder your life is constantly begging for happiness here, there and everywhere.

It is difficult to love mankind. It is difficult to devote ourselves to mankind. It is difficult to surrender ourselves to mankind. This is true. In the same way, it is difficult to love God, to serve God, to devote ouselves to God and to surrender our living breath to God. Why? The simple reason is that we want to possess and be possessed. We are constantly making ourselves victims of ignorance. That is to say, our desires can never be fulfilled. We have countless desires. God will fulfil only those desires that will be of some use, from which we will derive benefit. If He were to fulfil our countless desires, then He would be doing an injustice to our aspiring souls. That He will not do. He knows what is best for us and He has given us beyond our capacity, though unfortunately we are unaware of this.

God does not have to punish us
By blessing the heads
Of our countless desires.

Remind me, my Lord, from time to time, that You have taught me how to love the world unconditionally.

Each moment we are given ample opportunity to love mankind. If we really love mankind, then we want to offer devoted service to mankind. When we really want to enlarge our existence, expand our consciousness and be one, inseparably one, with the Vast, then surrender is the only answer. Each moment we see right in front of us a barrier between one human being and another—an adamantine wall between two people. We cannot communicate properly, wholeheartedly and soulfully. Why? Because we are wanting in love. Love is our inseparable oneness with the rest of the world, with God's entire creation. We can break asunder this adamantine wall on the strength of our soulful love.

Develop soulfully pure tears
Of oneness-love.
Then the universal life of beauty
Will be all yours.

You love your inner life. That means God has a very special concern for you.

You constantly surrender to earthly things—noise, traffic lights, the government. You feel that if you do not surrender to these things, you will be totally lost, whereas if you do surrender, at least you can maintain your existence on earth. If you want to lead an aspiring life, then you have to have this same kind of feeling toward spiritual things. You have to feel that if you do not pray, if you do not meditate, then you will be totally lost; if you do not cry, if you do not surrender to the higher divinity, then your whole existence will be of no value and you need not stay on earth. You have to feel that without the inner guidance you are totally helpless and lost. This inner guidance comes only when you really want to surrender your ignorance to the light within you.

Mine is not the way
To follow the world.
Mine is not the way
To lead the world.
Mine is the way
To walk along with God.

If you feel that it is not enough just to maintain your existence on earth, if you feel that your existence should have some meaning, some purpose, some fulfilment, then you have to go to the inner life, the spiritual life.

Aspiring people will try to go beyond earthly circumstances and events and surrender to their inner divinity. This is not the surrender of a slave to the master; it is not a helpless surrender. Here one surrenders his imperfections, limitations, bondage and ignorance to his highest Self, which is flooded with peace, light and bliss. Here one does not lose his individuality or personality. No! Rather his individuality and his personality are enlarged. They expand into Infinity.

He has experienced the beauty
Of his inner life.
Therefore he is happy.
He has now to surrender
The ugliness of his outer life
To his Beloved Supreme
So that both he and his Lord
Can be happy.

Brooding and despondency are the worst foes to kill life in all its divine inspiration. No more brooding, no more despondency. Your life shall become the beauty of a rose, the song of the dawn, the dance of the twilight.

We should not worry. We should have implicit faith in God, in our Inner Pilot. We have to feel that not only does God know what is best for us, but He will do what is best for us. We worry because we do not know what is going to happen to us tomorrow, or even the next minute. But if we can feel that there is someone who thinks of us infinitely more than we think of ourselves, and if we can consciously offer our responsibility to Him, saying, "You be responsible. Eternal Father, Eternal Mother, You be responsible for what I do and say and grow into," then our past, our present and our future become His problem. As long as we try to be responsible for our own life, we will be miserable. We will not be able to properly utilise even two minutes out of every twenty-four hours we have.

It is good to know
That God loves me.
It is better to know
That God needs me.
It is best to know
That God does everything
Unconditionally for me.

The world is strewn with difficulties. In a sense, it is full of thorns. But if you put on shoes, you can walk on the thorns. What are these shoes made of? They are made of God's Grace.

We should not and we need not ever worry about our destiny. On the strength of his surrender, a spiritual person becomes inseparably one with God's cosmic Will. Right now we do not surrender to God's Will, and that is why we suffer. We feel that if we do not do something for ourselves, then who is going to do it? But this is not true. There is someone who will do everything for us and that is our Inner Pilot. What is expected from us? Only conscious surrender to His Will. He will act in and through us only when we become His conscious instruments. When we can feel that we are the instruments and He is the Doer, then we will not worry about our destiny, we will not be afraid of our destiny. For we will know and feel that it is in the all-loving Hands of God, who will do everything in us, through us and for us.

Do not say
That you alone can do it.
Say that God does it in and through you.
Then lo, it is all done.

The aim of life is to become conscious of the Supreme Reality. The aim of life is to be the conscious expression of the Eternal Being.

Oneness is the only relationship that can forever last, because all human beings are either conscious or unconscious sharers of one divine and supreme Reality. For the unconscious sharers, dissatisfaction is the deplorable reality. If we are unconscious sharers, the body-consciousness separates us, the mental individuality separates us. But for the conscious sharers, there is only the psychic unity. If we are conscious sharers, the psychic unity awakens us, illumines us, fulfils us and immortalises us.

If you do not buy
Your mind's division-products,
God will grant you His Heart's
Illumination-Satisfaction-Feast.

When a sincere seeker prays and meditates, he radiates beauty. This beauty comes directly from his inner existence, his soul.

When we pray, we offer the beauty of our heart's intensity to the Supreme. When we meditate, we offer the beauty of our inner silence to the Supreme. When we love the outer world, knowing that the outer world is the manifestation and expression of the Supreme, then we offer the beauty of our universal oneness to the Supreme.

Your heart's surrender-shrine
Is the beauty unparalleled
That climbs up
To touch the core of Heaven.

As our very existence depends on God alone, we must be independent of the values of others, the opinions of others, the demands of others.

To detach yourself emotionally from irritating people and situations, first you have to identify yourself with the standards of the person who is creating the irritation. Suppose you are in your office and somebody is creating unnecessary problems. If you get angry with him, that will not solve the problem. Instead, you will be tortured inwardly by your anger and outwardly by the person. If you allow yourself to become angry, you will only lose your own inner strength. But if you come down to the standard of that person and identify with him, you will see that he himself is very unhappy and therefore wishes consciously or unconsciously to make others unhappy as well.

Is there any human being
Who is not the embodiment
Of opposing realities?

No happiness can be seen, no happiness can be felt, without the heart's peace-smile.

Another way to avoid becoming involved in irritating situations is to invoke peace. For the spiritual person, for the sincere seeker, it is always advisable to bring down peace from above. While invoking peace you will feel enormous strength inside you and around you. The power of inner peace is infinitely greater, more solid and concrete, than any other situation created by anybody on earth. Your inner peace can easily devour the irritation caused by somebody else.

How can we have peace?
Not by talking about peace,
But by walking
Along the road of peace.

JULY

Peace of mind
Cannot be obtained overnight.
To achieve peace of mind
We have to invest many silence-years
In spirituality.

Your loving heart is your inexhaustible wealth in your inner world.

A spiritual seeker uses his heart and his soul to see the world within and the world without. He does not use his outer eyes. He has seen time and again that the vision of his outer eyes is limited, precisely because this vision is guided by the subtle or unconscious operation of the unlit, unillumined mind. It is simply impossible for the outer eyes to identify themselves with the quintessence of beauty. But if we use the heart, immediately we become part and parcel of the substance and essence of what we are seeing.

The unaspiring mind thinks
That meditation is a waste of time.
The aspiring heart feels and knows
That meditation is
The secret and sacred blossoming
Of one's Heaven-ascending life.

Each time a birthday comes, mortal death knocks at our body's door. But the immortal soul inside the body-room calls out, "You are knocking at the wrong door. Go away, go away!"

I am a fool if I consciously live in the physical. I am a greater fool if I constantly admire and adore my physical body. I am the greatest fool if I live only to satisfy the needs of my physical existence. I am a wise person if I know that there is something called the soul. I am a wiser person if I care to see and feel my soul. I am the wisest person if I live in my soul and for my soul constantly and soulfully, unreservedly and unconditionally.

O body, my body,
Think of the soul.
For with the help of the soul
You will grow into
Eternity's poise, peace, light and bliss.

May the breath of spirituality become my life's only strength.

When the ego is operating, we feel that we are indispensable. We feel that we know better than everybody else and we are responsible for everything. We feel that everybody needs us. The transcendental Self houses the entire cosmos and offers liberation or freedom to each individual soul. The big 'I' is always extending itself. When we are consciously expanding, we drink in ecstasy. We expand like a bird spreading its wings. When we try to possess something, we try to possess it by hook or by crook. But the spontaneous expansion of our consciousness is like a mother spreading her arms around her children. There is no possessive feeling. We just feel that on the strength of our aspiration, we are extending our own inner reality.

Look up, look up!
His Cry is in you.
His Smile is for you.

Your heart must become a sea of love. Your mind must become a river of detachment.

Detachment is often misunderstood. We feel that if someone is detached, he is indifferent. We think that when we want to be detached from someone, we must show him utter indifference, to the point of total neglect. This is not true. When we are indifferent to someone, we do nothing for him. We have nothing to do with his joy or sorrow, his achievement or failure. But when we are truly detached, we work for him devotedly and selflessly, and offer the results of our actions at the Feet of the Lord Supreme, our Inner Pilot.

In my attachment
I learn from man
And his ignorance-night.
In my detachment
I learn from God
And His Compassion-Sun.

Do you know the secret of my spiritual success? I have freed myself from the past. I live in constant, unending newness of life.

How can we grow into God? We must be ready every day to change, and not to remain prisoners of the past. When today is over we have to feel that it is past. It will not be of any help to us in growing into the Highest Supreme. No matter how sweet, how loving or how fulfilling the past was, it cannot give us anything now that we do not already have. We are moving forward towards the goal, so no matter how satisfying the past was, we have to feel that it is only a prison. The seed grows into a plant, and then it becomes a huge tree. If the consciousness of the plant remains in the seed, then there will be no further manifestation. Yes, we shall remain grateful to the seed, because it enabled us to grow into a plant. But we will not pay much attention to the seed stage. Once we have become a plant, let our aim be to become a tree. Always we have to look forward towards the goal. Only when we become the tallest tree will our full satisfaction dawn.

Let yesterday sleep,
And allow not frustration
To rule your mind.
Tomorrow's satisfaction-sun
Will be all yours.
Just start seeing the rise
Of your surrender-heart-tide.

By seeing the past I gain nothing. By knowing the future I gain something. By living in the present I gain everything.

We must always remain in the present. This present is constantly ready to bring the golden future into our heart. Today's achievement is most satisfactory, but we have to feel that today's achievement is nothing in comparison to what tomorrow's achievement will be. Each time satisfaction dawns, we have to feel that this satisfaction is nothing in comparison to the satisfaction that is about to dawn. We have to feel that every second brings new life, new growth, new opportunity. If we are ready to allow change into our life at every second, every minute, every day, we are bound to grow.

Sing not soulful songs
With your yesterday's mind.
Sing fruitful songs
With your today's heart.

Man has two weapons: hope and despair. With hope he tries to kill the stagnation of incapacity. With despair he can kill the birth of the golden future.

We will own peace only after we have totally stopped finding fault with others. We have to feel the whole world as our very own. When we observe others' mistakes, we enter into their imperfections. This does not help us in the least. Strangely enough, the deeper we plunge, the clearer it becomes to us that the imperfections of others are our own imperfections, but in different bodies and minds. Whereas if we think of God, His Compassion and His Divinity enlarge our inner vision of Truth. We must come in the fulness of our spiritual realisation to accept humanity as one family.

Even for a fleeting second
Offer good will to others.
Your good thoughts
Are significant contributions
To the Supreme in humanity.

**Past defeats, past pains and past humilia-
tions can never match the delights of your
present victory-crown.**

We must not allow our past to torment and
destroy the peace of our heart. Our present good
and divine actions can easily counteract our bad
and undivine actions of the past. If sin has the
power to make us weep, meditation undoubtedly
has the power to give us joy, to endow us with
divine wisdom.

*The moment he turned his back
On the past,
The golden dawn
Of tomorrow's silence-beauty
Invited him to ride
In the chariot of the transcendental Sun-God.*

**A full harvest of peace I collected the day I
realised that neither earth's great hunger
nor Heaven's good feast desires my eager
presence.**

Peace comes to us and we lose it because we
feel that we are not responsible for humanity, or
that we are not part and parcel of humanity. We
have to feel that God and humanity are like a
great tree. God is the tree, and the branches are
His manifestation. We are branches, and there
are many other branches. All these branches are
part of the tree and are one with each other and
with the tree. If we can feel that we have the
same relationship with God and with humanity
as the branch has with its fellow branches and
with the tree as a whole, we are bound to get
everlasting peace.

There are two medicines
To give you peace of mind:
"I am everything"
And
"This world does not belong to me."
Use one of the two.

Character is just what we inwardly are and outwardly do.

When you have to defend yourself or protect yourself, try to use a higher weapon. If people say something and you retaliate on the same level, there will be no end to it. Again, if you simply swallow your anger they will continue to take advantage of you. But when they see and feel tremendous inner peace in you, they will see something in you which can never be conquered. They will see a change in you, and this change will not only puzzle them but also threaten and frighten them. They will feel that their weapons are useless.

If your aspiration is genuine,
Then it will save you
At every moment
From world-complaints.

Peace is the most effective weapon with which to conquer injustice.

When you pray and meditate, your whole being becomes flooded with peace. Then no matter what other people do, you will just feel that they are your own children playing in front of you. You will say, "These are all children. What more can I expect from them?" But right now, because they are grown up in terms of years, you become angry and upset instead. If you pray and meditate regularly, you will soon feel that your peace is infinitely stronger, more fulfilling and more energising than the unfortunate situation that others may create.

This world of ours
Is full of sharp criticism-arrows.
These arrows cannot hurt
The peace-illumined mind
And God-intoxicated heart.

What do we get from the inner life? We get simplicity, sincerity, integrity, purity, humility and divinity. He who has all these divine qualities will, without fail, have a life of joy, peace, freedom and fulfilment. And he who does not have these divine qualities will unmistakably have a life of tears, turmoil, bondage and frustration.

From the inner life we get a growing, flowing and energising consciousness to illumine and perfect our thoughts and feelings and to accomplish our aims. We can also grow into active and effective participants in God's cosmic experience. To live an inner life is to become fully conscious of God's existence. To become fully conscious of God's existence is to love humanity's breath with a boundless heart. The divine harmony is and can be established in one's inner and outer nature only when one accepts the inner life as a source of constant inspiration to guide, mould and shape the outer life.

Life's battlefield
Will be all peace
When the sound of the mind
Gives way
To the silence of the heart.

Self-love and self-hatred are two diseases that can be cured by one medicine, and that medicine is God-love.

We want to please the world, but how can we please the world if we are not pleased with our own lives? It is sheer absurdity to try to please others if we are not pleased with our inner and outer existence. God has given us big mouths and we try to please others with our mouths, but inside our hearts there is a barren desert. If we have no aspiration, how can we offer the world peace, joy and love? How can we offer anything divine when we do not practise what we preach? Spirituality offers us the capacity to practise what we preach. If we do not follow the path of spirituality, we shall only preach; it will be a one-sided game. Our preaching will bear fruit only when it is practised.

To uplift the earth-atmosphere,
Start from today
With the heart that gives
And the life that surrenders.

In life there are many questions, but surrender to God's Will is the only answer.

How can we fulfil all our responsibilities? We have tried in human ways, but we have failed. We think of the world with good thoughts and ideas, but the world remains exactly the same as it was yesterday. We love the world, but the world still remains full of cruelty and hatred. We try to please the world, but the world does not want to be pleased. It is as if the world has taken a vow that it will not allow itself to be pleased. And why does all this happen? It is because we have not pleased our Inner Pilot, the one we have to please first. If we have no aspiration to please our Inner Pilot, how can we offer the world peace, joy and love? Unless and until we have pleased the Inner Pilot, the world will always remain a battlefield where the soldiers of fear, doubt, anxiety, worry, imperfection, limitation and bondage will fight; and consciously or unconsciously we will play with these undivine soldiers. Fear, doubt, anxiety and worry can never offer us world peace.

Look deep within.
Are you expecting God
To please you in your own way?
If that is what you want,
You and your life
Will be total failures.

As a flower is blessed with fragrance and beauty, even so each human being is blessed with inner purity and divinity.

Deep within us divinity is crying to come to the fore. There the divine soldiers are our simplicity, sincerity, purity, humility and feeling of oneness. These soldiers are more than ready and eager to fight with fear, doubt, anxiety and worry. Unfortunately, we are not consciously identifying ourselves with the divine soldiers. We are consciously or unconsciously identifying ourselves with the undivine soldiers, and that is why world peace is still a far cry. World peace can be achieved, revealed, offered and manifested on earth when the divine power of love replaces the undivine love of power.

Make new inner friends:
Purity, humility and divinity
Are waiting for your invitation.

True happiness lies in self-giving to the Supreme inside you—only there; no other place.

Why do we work? We work to support ourselves, to support our dear ones. We may also work to keep our bodies in perfect condition. A true aspirant looks upon work as a veritable blessing. To him, work is nothing short of dedicated service. He has discovered the truth that by offering the results of what he says, does and thinks, he will be able to realise God. He works for the sake of God. He lives for the sake of God. He realises Divinity for the sake of God.

Be not interested
In receiving credit from God.
Be only interested
In serving God.

We have to be wise. We can use each moment for a divine purpose. We can use each moment in performing our soulful duty.

Duty is painful, tedious and monotonous simply because we do it with our ego, pride and vanity. Duty is pleasant, encouraging and inspiring when we do it for God's sake. What we need is to change our attitude toward duty. If we work for the sake of God, then there is no duty. All is joy. All is beauty. Each action has to be performed and offered at the Feet of God. Duty for God's sake is the duty supreme.

Love your family much.
This is your great duty.
Love mankind more.
This is your greater duty.
Love God most.
This is your greatest duty,
The duty supreme.

Work soulfully. Lo, you will not be able to find any difference between Heaven and earth.

A spiritual person has found his work. His work is selfless service. His work is dedicated action. Indeed, he has no need of any other blessedness. His action is the divine acceptance of earthly existence. And for this he needs a perfect body, a strong mind, a soulful heart and a supremely inspired life of inner receptivity and outer capacity. Action is entering into the battlefield of life. Action is conquering life's untold miseries and teeming limitations. Action is transforming life's devouring imperfection into glowing perfection. Action is something infinitely deeper and higher than the mere survival of physical existence. Action is the secret supreme, which enables us to enter into the Life Eternal.

There is no such thing
As insignificant work.
Therefore, we must needs do everything
With our heart's love
And our life's respect.

If your mind is intent on your life's transformation, then yours will be a world-home of peace.

According to some people, human life is just a cruel, meaningless and hopeless four-letter word: work. I wish to say that they are mistaken. They like work; what they hate is the sense of labour, the burden of labour. Labour and favour perfectly rhyme. After all, whose favour is it? God's favour. Indeed, he is God's chosen child, and he alone is God's favourite, who works to please God. And in pleasing God, he realises and fulfils himself. Then he tells the world that human life is a divinely meaningful three-letter word: joy.

For an unaspiring man,
Work is punishment,
Work is torture.
For an aspiring man,
Work is a blessing,
Work is a joy.

I love to converse with God. He is such a charming conversationalist, and I am a charmed listener.

There can be no greater choice or higher prize than to listen to the inner voice. If we willfully refuse to listen to the inner voice, our false gains will lead us to an inevitable loss. If we listen soulfully to the inner voice, our true gains will not only protect us from imminent destruction but will surprisingly hasten our realisation of the transcendental Truth.

To reap the richest harvest
Of my aspiration-heart,
I shall listen
To the silence-flooded whispers
Of my Inner Pilot.

An aspirant must realise that the inner voice is not a gift, but an achievement. The more soulfully he strives for it, the sooner he unmistakably owns it.

The inner voice is at once man's untiring guide and his true friend. If a man goes deep within, the inner voice will tell him what to do. If he goes deeper, the inner voice will tell him how to do it. If he goes deeper, the inner voice will give him the capacity. If he goes still deeper, the inner voice will convince him that he is doing the right thing in the right way.

My Lord Supreme,
Would You kindly make
All important decisions in my life?
I shall always ask You
Inwardly and outwardly what I should do.
My Lord,
Do make all decisions
In my life.

There is a word that is very sweet, pure and familiar to us. This word is conscience. Conscience is another name for the inner voice.

Conscience can live in two places: in the heart of truth and in the mouth of falsehood. When conscience strikes us once, we must think that it is showing us its unconditional love. When it strikes us twice, we must feel that it is showing us its unreserved concern. When it strikes us thrice, we must realise that it is offering us its boundless compassion to prevent us from diving deep into the sea of ignorance.

I know both your sweet,
Encouraging and inspiring secrets.
You are happy because
You have uprooted your desire-tree.
You are perfect because
You always obey the commands
Of your inner monitor:
Conscience-light.

Love is the secret key to open God's Door.

If love means to possess someone or something, then that is not real love, not pure love. If love means to give oneself, to become one with everything and everyone, then that is real love. Real love is total oneness with the object loved and with the Possessor of love. And who is the Possessor of love? God. Without love, we cannot become one with God. Love is the inner bond, the inner connection, the inner link between man and God, between the finite and the Infinite.

A joyful God-seeker
Will definitely be able
To meet with God,
The playful Lover.

There is no such thing as sweetness-expectation, for inside expectation there are always desire-thorns.

Man has countless desires. When his desires are not fulfilled, he curses himself; he feels that he is a failure, hopeless and helpless. He wants to prove his existence on earth with the fruits of his desires. He thinks that by fulfilling his desires he will be able to prove himself superior to others. Yet, alas, he fails, he has failed and he shall fail. But God comes to him and says, "My child, you have not failed. You are not hopeless. You are not helpless. How can you be hopeless? I am growing in you with My ever-luminous and ever-fulfilling Dream. How can you be helpless? I am inside you as infinite power."

When we do not seek to dominate,
We can be happy.
When we do not expect,
We can be perfect.

We have to feel that we embody infinite light, infinite truth and infinite bliss and that now we have to reveal and manifest these divine qualities.

The supreme Goal is within. The Goal is crying for us, but we are looking for it elsewhere, where it does not exist. We cry for our own existence, which is full of fear, doubt, ignorance, pride, vanity and selfishness. But if we cried for God every day, if we meditated early in the morning for harmony, peace, bliss, plenitude and fulfilment, then we would see, feel, realise and grow into our Goal. We would discover that our transcendental Goal is within and grow into its very image.

The logic of the seeker's faith:
His life exists precisely because
His God exists.

Who told you that you are unworthy? It is absolutely untrue! You are already in God's Vision-Boat, and He is piloting the Boat cheerfully and proudly.

Let us try to know ourselves. Let us try to observe what we truly are. Very often we feel that we are insignificant creatures. We have nowhere to go, nothing to achieve and nothing to give. This is what we feel in our day-to-day existence. But what we truly are is totally different from what we feel. We are all God's children. At each moment, God is pouring into us something divine and something truthful. He expects much from us, but nothing beyond our capacity. He knows what we can consciously offer to Him. Right now, we feel that we are weak, unimportant, useless. But in God's Eyes, we are divine, we are fruitful, we are infinite.

Little soulful efforts
Can make not only a good seeker
But also a perfect instrument of God.

If you want to understand yourself, then do not examine yourself. Just love yourself more sincerely, more soulfully and more self-givingly.

I love myself. What do I love about myself? Not my body. If I love my body for the sake of my body, tomorrow I shall be frustrated because there are millions and billions of human beings on earth who are more beautiful than I am. Naturally I will feel miserable. If I love my physical mind for the sake of my mind, tomorrow I shall see millions and billions of mental giants right in front of me, and my mental capacity will fade into insignificance. If I love my vital dynamism for the sake of my vital dynamism, then I shall see that there are millions and billions of people who are simply inundated with striking dynamism. Similarly, if I love anything else of my own for its own sake, I am bound to be frustrated. I shall defeat my own divine purpose. But if I love myself just because God is expressing Himself through this body, vital, mind and heart, then I see that I am unique and peerless in the whole history of the universe, because no other individual is going to be created by God with the same capacities, the same understanding, or the same experiences.

A heart of love
Has to be used
Always for a sacred purpose.

If you know how to love yourself divinely, you will be able to save yourself from being loved by others undivinely.

Each individual can love himself just because he is a direct channel of the Divine. God wants to express Himself in each individual in a unique way. When we become consciously and fully one with God, we not only fulfil Him, but we also fulfil ourselves. When I say that I really and truly love myself because I love Truth, it means that I consciously feel that Truth is constantly breathing in me, with me and for me.

Do not belittle your aspiration-cry.
That is the job others are dying to do.
Love yourself more divinely.
This is the job you alone can
And you alone must do.

Nothing is as beautiful in man as his heart's sincerity.

Sincerity can be developed. It can be developed like a muscle. There are some people who are naturally sincere, and others who are naturally insincere. Those who are sincere from the dawn of their lives are blessed. But those who are insincere need not and must not curse themselves. They can be sincere if they want to. The moment they truly want to be sincere, God in His infinite Compassion will help them. With His deepest Joy, Pride and Concern He will help them.

When I am sincerity incarnate,
I try to save my life from myself.
When I am insincerity incarnate,
I proudly dare to save
The entire world.

Your power of self-control is the tree of eternal freedom.

In the spiritual life, self-control is most important, significant and fruitful. No self-control, no self-realisation. In the dictionary we come across hundreds of thousands of words. Of all these words, self-control is the most difficult one to practise. How can we have self-control? If we want to have self-control, we have to surrender ourselves to the Source. This Source is Light; this Source is God.

If you are really great and good,
Then every day you must highly appreciate
Your dedication-life,
For it has given you
The power of self-control.
And to your extreme joy and satisfaction,
Nobody else but you yourself
Has command over you.

A self-controlled life will guarantee salvation.

Unfortunately, we are living in an age when self-control is not appreciated. It has become an object of ridicule. A man is trying hard for self-mastery. His friends, neighbours, relatives and acquaintances all mock at him. They find no reality in his sincere attempt to master his life. They think that the way they are living their lives is more worthwhile. The man who is trying to control his life is a fool, according to them. But who is the fool—he who wants to conquer himself or he who is constantly a victim of fear, doubt, worry and anxiety? Needless to say, he who wants to conquer himself is not only the wisest man but the greatest divine hero.

If you struggle to control yourself,
God will smilingly help you enroll
In His life-transformation-school.

AUGUST

Every day cultivate adamantine will
In the depths of your heart
So that with no difficulty you can bestride
All your problems in the mental world.

To strive to do something unique is undoubtedly good, but it is better to know whether that unique thing is what God wants you to do.

Our human ego wants to do something great, grand and magnificent. But this unique thing need not be the thing that God wants us to do. It is always nice to be able to do great things, but perhaps God has not chosen us to do that particular thing. God may have chosen us to do something insignificant in the outer world. In the Eye of God, he is the greatest devotee who performs his God-ordained duty soulfully and devotedly, no matter how insignificant it may seem. Each person is a chosen child of God. Similarly, each person is destined to play a significant part in God's divine Game. But each person has to know what God wants from him. When one becomes aware of God's plan for him, then he abides by God's decision. When God sees that particular person performing the role that He chose for him, then only will God be filled with divine pride. Our ego will try to achieve and to perform great things, but in God's Eye we can never be great unless and until we do what God wants us to do.

Surrender to God's Will
And become an unconditional
God-lover.
Do it! You can!
Lo, you have already done it.

Unconditional surrender is the immortal birth of a genuine God-lover.

At one moment our ego will make us feel that we are nothing and at the next moment our ego will make us feel that we are everything. We have to be very careful of both our feelings of importance and our feelings of unimportance. We have to say that if God wants us to be nothing, then we will gladly be nothing, and if God wants us to be everything, we will be everything gladly. We have to surrender unconditionally and cheerfully to the Will of God.

You may not know the best way
To please God,
But if you pray daily
To be able to please Him
In His own way,
Your prayer will unmistakably
One day bear fruit.

The human ego is constantly bothering us. But if we have the divine ego which makes us feel, "I am God's son, I am God's daughter," we will not separate our existence from the rest of God's creation.

God is omniscient, omnipotent, omnipresent. If He is all, if He is everywhere and if I am His child, how can I be limited to one particular place? This divine ego or divine pride is absolutely necessary. "I cannot wallow in the pleasures of ignorance. I am God's child. To realise Him, to discover Him in myself and in everyone is my birthright. He is my Father. If He is so divine, then what is wrong with me? I came from Him, from the Absolute, from the Supreme; therefore, I should be divine too." This kind of divine pride has to come forward. The ordinary ego that binds us constantly has to be transformed. The divine ego, the divine pride, which claims the universe as its very own, should be our only choice.

Imaginative I was,
Intuitive I have become,
Receptive I shall be.
And then I shall claim God
Exactly the way
God has always claimed me.

Be sleeplessly on the alert. Your ego-life can easily keep growing without nourishment.

The easiest way to conquer ego is to offer gratitude to God for five minutes daily. If you cannot offer gratitude for five minutes, then offer it for one minute. Offer your gratitude to God. Then you will feel that inside you a sweet, fragrant and beautiful flower is growing. That is the flower of humility. When you offer Him your gratitude, God gives you something most beautiful, which is humility. When you discover the flower of humility inside you, you will feel that your consciousness has covered the length and breadth of the universe.

A true God-server knows
That his heart's gratitude-speed
Is infinitely faster
Than anything else in God's entire creation.

The human life itself is a strong desire to be led by the clever mind.

We have to pray to God constantly to come to the fore in us. Let Him guide us and mould us in His own way, into His very image. We are not the doers. We have to feel that we are the instruments and He is the player. If we have that kind of feeling, then we can always be happy. If we feel that we are God's instruments and that we are helpless unless God acts in and through us, naturally He will do the right thing in and through us. The right thing for whom? For us. But we have to consciously give Him the chance. We shall give Him this chance soulfully, devotedly and unconditionally. We will say to God, "Take care of us. We came from You. We want You to look after us now."

The choice lies with you.
Either you take full responsibility
For your life
Or let God manifest Himself
In and through you
In His own way.

Do not forget to ask your mind and heart every day, without fail, how you can please God in His own way.

When you please God in God's own way, you have played your part. When you have done something for God in God's own way, your heart will expand to such an extent that you will be able to see all your friends, even your so-called enemies, inside your own heart. But if you please God in your own way, divine satisfaction will not be found inside your heart. When you try to please God in your own way, you may deceive yourself into feeling that you have pleased God, but actually you have pleased only your ego. When you please your own ego, you will not really be able to please anyone else on earth. But if you please God divinely, you will see satisfaction even in your worst enemy.

If you can repeat from morn to eve,
"My Lord Supreme,
I want to please You
In Your own way,"
Then you cannot
Unconsciously disobey God.

One can overcome the ego and have total humility if one can feel constantly that he is not indispensable, that only God is indispensable.

God is constantly standing in front of each of us as a golden opportunity. One has to feel that this opportunity is the only thing that he needs. If he feels that God needs him for a particular purpose which he alone can fulfil, then he is totally lost. One has to feel that his spiritual aspiration itself is the greatest blessing that he can receive from God. There are billions of people on earth who do not care for the spiritual life, who are still spiritually fast asleep. Why is it that one particular individual is conscious of the spiritual life while the others are still sleeping? The moment one is conscious of the spiritual life, he has to feel that he has received the greatest boon from God.

God will prove your importance
To the world
The day you can sincerely feel
That you are not indispensable
Either in this world or in any world.

A self-giving life is a special blessing-message that lives forever on earth.

If we receive even an iota of inner peace or bliss, we will feel that life on earth is fulfilling. Whatever else we have or we are is absolutely worthless in God's Eye. Only if mental brilliance, material wealth and physical power are placed in the service of the Divine do they become meaningful. The divine light gives them a new life. Without spiritual wealth, outer wealth is totally useless. So let us be very humble in our spiritual life and give utmost importance to the spiritual treasures: purity, love, devotion and surrender. Only when we have these can our outer wealth and power be utilised in a divine way.

Be spontaneous like a child.
A child does not try
To acquire anything unnatural.
He does not try to be somebody
Or something else.
He approaches God in a natural way.

**The human ego can never, under any cir-
cumstances experience true inner joy. The
human ego may experience pleasure in
accomplishing many things, in accumulating
wealth and in achieving power over others.
But true inner joy is self-created. It does not
depend on outer circumstances or outer
achievements.**

The ego, which is the little 'I', is constantly seeking something other than itself because it is limited. The very nature of the ego is to be dissatisfied and displeased. It is never satisfied with what
it has and what it is because the truth is always
somewhere else. The truth is far away from the
ego, but the ego thinks it is just around the cor-
ner, near at hand, within its easy reach. Wherever
the ego is, it seems to be standing on one shore
of a river and seeing that truth is on the other
shore. Then, when it goes to that shore, it discov-
ers that truth is somewhere else after all. The
small 'I' is always enamoured of its own concep-
tion of truth. Although it is walking in the field of
discouraging experiences, it feels that it is about
to enter into the field of encouraging and satisfying experiences.

Do you want to possess the world?
Then do the first thing first.
Pray to God
To possess you entirely,
Along with your mind's desire-forest.

Ego feeds on attention. The perfection of our precarious animal-human nature feeds on God's Compassion-Sea.

If someone feels that by fulfilling the ego's demands the ego will be exhausted, as we exhaust our money by spending it, then he is mistaken. If we have money, we use it and then it is gone. In the case of the ego, it is not like that. It goes on and on. Ignorance is the mother of the ego. As there is no end to our ignorance until we aspire, so also there is no limit to our ego. On the contrary, if we feed it by fulfilling its demands, it will only grow stronger and stronger. If one really wants to have a life of inner joy and fulfilment, then ego, the thief, has to be caught, and the sooner the better. This thief constantly steals our inner divine qualities: our joy, our peace, our feeling of oneness with the rest of the world.

Conceal your self-interest-cry.
God's Satisfaction-Smile
Will in no time
Enlighten you.

Oneness with unaspiring people means dining with death. Oneness with aspiring people means dancing with God.

When you are with somebody who has a strong ego, you will consciously or unconsciously be influenced by it. How? By its unlit, obscure, arrogant, aggressive power. His ego will try to make you his slave. While he tries to make you the slave of his ego, from deep within you your own ego will come forward to resist him. After a few months or a few years you will try to exercise your own ego by making somebody else your slave. He is fulfilling his ego by exercising it on you, and you will try to fulfil your ego by exercising it on somebody else, because this is what you have learned from him. But by exercising one's ego one can never be happy and satisfied. Outwardly he can make you feel or make himself feel that he is happy, but inwardly he never feels happy. By exercising one's ego nobody can be happy.

You cannot be both
At the same time:
Your mind's oversized ego-tree
And
Your heart's small happiness-plant.

Never give any importance to the ego that wants to compete with others.

You have to feel your oneness with everybody. When you do, immediately you will expand your consciousness. If someone does something well, immediately you have to feel that it is you who have done it. He should also do the same thing when you do something significant. Whenever any individual does something very well, others have to feel that it is their conscious inspiration and aspiration that have enabled that individual to achieve this success. If we always have an attitude of teamwork, then we will be able to conquer the ego.

When you show no interest whatsoever
In ego-competition,
You at once win
Both God's Crown and God's Throne.

O doubt! Unreasonable is your existence-reality. What is worse, you have stayed with my mind far beyond my imagination.

Why do we doubt? Doubt enters into us because we are not certain of our achievements, of our accomplishments, or of what we will do in the near and distant future. If we doubt others, we are not doing something really harmful. But if we doubt ourselves, we are doing something most damaging. The moment we doubt ourselves, we weaken our possibility and ruin our potentiality. The tree which we can become will die while it is still a plant from lack of nourishment.

How can you succeed?
Can you not see
That your mind is lost
In yesterday's failures
And that you are losing your heart
In tomorrow's doubts?

In the spiritual life there is only one rule, and that is to have faith.

Faith is like a muscle: it can be developed. As we develop our muscles if we exercise regularly, we can also exercise and increase our inner capacity. God does not bring anybody into the world without giving him capacity. Through regular practice we can become inwardly strong. If we concentrate and meditate soulfully and sincerely each morning, then doubt cannot play its destructive role in us. As we become stronger in our inner life, we will be able to say, "Let doubt attack me. I shall be able to maintain my perfect faith."

Unless and until you move
Out of the doubt-neighbourhood,
God will not appear
Before you
And will not introduce Himself
To you.

The secret of inner success is constancy to our highest character.

When you enter the spiritual life, sometimes you see and feel many undivine qualities suddenly come to the fore. Do not think that weaknesses and imperfections are coming to the fore in you just because you have accepted the spiritual life. On the contrary, they were there before, but they were hidden. You should be grateful to your spiritual life for bringing your imperfections to the fore. The sooner your imperfections come to the fore, the sooner you will be able to face them and conquer them. So when doubt and other imperfections attack you, you should say, "You have come. Now let me conquer you once and for all. Then I will be free."

Be not afraid
Of your teeming imperfections.
Weep not bitterly,
For the divine hero in you
Will soon come to the fore.

Try to explore the limits of aspiration. God will give you the power of His self-giving Smile.

God will never be satisfied unless and until each individual has realised Him. That is His Will. But it is a long, arduous process. Today somebody becomes perfect, tomorrow somebody else becomes perfect, and the day after, a third person becomes perfect. God's Cosmic Game has to be consciously played by everyone. And in this Cosmic Game, everybody has to become perfect. Unless and until everybody becomes perfect, God's Game will never be completed. Just because it is difficult, we can not say that we shall not be able to complete the Game.

If your progress in one field
Is obstructed,
Go another way.
There are so many ways open to you
If you look within.
Only do not give up
The idea of progress.

Only one piece of advice I have for you: never stop once you have started!

When we become conscious seekers, devoted seekers, unconditional seekers, we accelerate our spiritual progress. Then God-realisation does not remain a far cry. But we have to start. Something seems difficult when we have not consciously started. Once we consciously start something, we have to know that that thing will not always remain difficult. If we start something unconsciously today, tomorrow we will not know that we actually started and, after a while, we may totally forget about the thing. But if today we pray to God soulfully and consciously, and if tomorrow we again do it consciously and soulfully, and if we continue in this way, then nothing will remain difficult.

Your God-search
Is accelerating.
Therefore, God Himself
Is celebrating
Your graduation in Heaven.

Every day there is only one thing to learn: how to be honestly happy.

It is always best to be sincerely happy. That is the goal. Let us cry for happiness. If you are sincerely unhappy, use the antidote. Be more spiritual. Increase your inner cry. Then your unhappiness will be illumined. Your inner cry will make your unhappiness go away. But do not stick to false happiness. Like a false coin it will be detected. Even you yourself will catch it.

If you are devoted to depression,
You cannot be a student
At God's earth-transformation-school.

The significance of life is the constant presence of inner courage.

To remain happy in the face of obstacles, make progress. Just because there are hurdles, will you give up the race? Between you and the goal there may be a few obstacles, but you have to overcome them. If you say, "I do not want to overcome the obstacles, but I want to reach the goal," how can you expect to do it? If you are just at the starting point, you have to be prepared to encounter difficulties. When you have to cross a difficult hurdle, you will see whether you really want to reach the goal or not.

Your sterling faith in God
Can easily brave
Numberless buffets.

Delete from your conscious and unconscious memory the pangs of your past failure-life.

What is a mistake after all? If we think that a mistake means something that is to be followed by punishment, then we are totally wrong. First of all, let us take it as a failure. What is failure? Failures are the pillars of success. Let us take failure as God's experience in us. God is constantly experiencing Himself in us and through us. At the same time, He is running and carrying us towards the ultimate Goal of perfection. Let us take mistakes as half truths. If we take them as something abominable and unpardonable, then they will never be rectified or shaped into truth. But if we consider mistakes as imperfect or infinitesimal truths, if we see in a mistake an iota of truth, only then can we feel that the mistake can be rectified and transformed into truth.

> *You say to God,*
> *"Father, I have failed."*
> *God says to you,*
> *"Are you so sure, My son?"*
> *You say to God,*
> *"Father, I have succeeded!"*
> *God says to you,*
> *"My son, I am not so sure."*

Do not ridicule the sad failures of others. Who knows, you too may be sailing in the same boat before long!

The very idea of considering a mistake as something shameful or unmentionable creates a wrong vibration. We should always identify ourselves with our largest part, with the all-embracing part that includes the whole world, the entire humanity. At that time our so-called mistake is not a mistake. Then we feel that it is only an imperfection. It is a game of imperfection that we have played unconsciously but not deliberately. Instead, what we actually do is separate ourselves from the mistake as if it were something dirty, obscene and so ugly that we cannot touch it. With this approach we will never make progress. Instead, let us take the mistake as a lump of clay. This lump of clay can easily be shaped or moulded into a different form. Then, if we have wisdom enough, light enough, we can use that form for various purposes.

God asks you
Only for one favour:
Not to try to remember
Your past failure-life.

God does not believe in a failure-life. Therefore, how can you and I ever fail?

Instead of taking each mistake as a curse, we can take it as a blessing. First of all, we should not commit any mistakes consciously and deliberately. But if a mistake takes place in our inner nature, in our vital nature, in our physical nature, in our outer mind or physical mind, then immediately we should be ready to confess it to ourselves and to God. Confession is our immediate emancipation. Otherwise, we shall grow into a mountain of mistakes. The moment we have the courage to confess our mistake, God's adamantine Protection runs toward us. His Protection shelters us. His Protection immediately becomes our haven.

Do not allow yourself
To be devoured by past mistakes,
For God is expecting from your life
A profound inner transformation.

Be simple, be sincere, be pure and be humble. Go back, go back once more to the basics of your inner life.

Sometimes we enter into the inner life out of temptation. As people enter into the outer life to fulfil their desires, so also people practice the inner life for a few days or a few months. Then after they have tried, they feel that the inner life will not fulfil their desires. The worldly life is better for that. The inner life is difficult only when one wants to fulfil the outer life first and the inner life last. One has to fulfil the inner life first, or take both the inner life and the outer life together with the feeling that if the inner life is fed, then the outer life will automatically be nourished.

My morning promise:
Today I shall not fail God.
My evening promise:
Tomorrow I shall become
An infinitely better instrument
Of God.

What my mind needs is a fresh breeze of sweet hope to once more succeed gloriously in my life.

Oneness is the only reality. He who has established oneness with God has no insecurity. But until that oneness is established, the seeker has to be very careful. He must always remember that he has come here to become God's perfect instrument. Every hour and every day he should think, "Let me become a perfect instrument." Even if he is appreciated highly in the outer world, he should not have a complacent feeling. If he does, he will not strive to become better and he will not make any progress.

God is not interested
In knowing your outer weaknesses.
He is not interested
Even in your inner weaknesses.
He is only interested
In your outer and inner
Oneness with Him.

Ambition does not know that it shows us the way to an unsatisfied greatness.

Name, fame, earthly prosperity and earthly achievements will always prove to be useless, useless, useless, even for those who are not sincere seekers. There comes a time when even an ordinary human being will not hesitate to say that earthly achievements all end in frustration. The possessions and the achievements of the desire-life will always end in frustration. Only one thing has the capacity to give satisfaction and that is oneness—conscious, constant, complete, unreserved and unconditional oneness with the Will of the Supreme.

Pray to God
And meditate on God
Every day
To use you in His own way
So that He does not see you
As one of the countless
Useless human lives.

**If you can silence the mind and ask the heart
to speak to God, then only are you heading
in the right direction.**

Is there anybody who does not know the Will of
the Supreme? No! If you remain in the heart, at
every moment you will know what God's Will is.
But if you remain in the mind, never, never will
you be able to know the Will of the Supreme. You
may have grandiose thoughts and lofty ideas, but
they will not be the Will of the Supreme. Life's
victory or defeat, life's acceptance or rejection,
are not the ultimate reality in the Eye of the Supreme. He laughs at our acceptance or rejection
of life, at our victories and defeats. But He
triumphantly smiles at us when His Will becomes
our will. We do not have to become great in the
outer world to prove to the world or to Him that
we are worthy instruments of His. Never does he
care for our earthly status. He cares only for one
thing: our constant oneness with His Will.

You do your work:
You go on creating a new world.
God will ask the citizens
Of the old world
To applaud you, along with Him.

If we give importance to a thing, then automatically that thing becomes real to us. The moment we take away the importance of a thing, that thing has no value. If we really value the inner life, then the inner life has to become real.

When we do not pray and meditate, we see only the physical world around us. We feel that this is absolutely real. But when we pray and meditate, we see and feel that there is another world and that this physical world is only an expression of that world. But again, we have to know that we ourselves are the creator of this physical world. The physical world we build with our hands, with our outer capacities. The inner world we build with our will-power—not mere thought-power, but will-power.

Go forward
With your volcanic will-power!
Otherwise,
Yours will be a life
Of huge destruction.

The inner life teaches us how to be detached from the desire-life and how to be attached only to God.

How can we feel that the inner world is more real? The reality of something depends on the importance or value we give to it. Reality depends on necessity. If we are hungry, immediately food becomes the only reality before us, around us, within us, without us. Anything that demands our attention or concentration has to be real, whether it is material food or inner peace, light and delight. The reality of a thing depends on how necessary it is for us. If we need something, then that very thing has to become real.

> *Explore the secrets of the outer world.*
> *Implore the secrets of the inner world.*
> *Lo, the realities of the outer world*
> *Will at once be at your disposal,*
> *And the realities of the inner world*
> *Will extol you to the skies.*

Simplicity shortens the road that leads to God-discovery.

Simplicity embodies tremendous power. When we enter into the spiritual life, we can value this most significant achievement. We have countless desires. But from our list, if we can take out one desire, then to that extent our life becomes simple. When it becomes simple, an iota of peace dawns in our mental firmament. Each time we become simple, simpler, simplest, our desire-life becomes short, shorter, shortest. Then we enjoy peace of mind, light and delight.

Be a simple life.
Earth needs your help.
Be a pure heart.
Heaven needs your help.

God is in everything; that is why everything is divine.

With our aspiration we have to see how much divinity everything has. God is inside everything, but in the field of manifestation we have to know how much divinity a chair has and how much divinity a spiritual Master has. When one is wise one will see divinity infinitely more in a spiritual man than in a mad elephant. So in our life of aspiration, we have to be careful when we mix with people. We have to approach the person or thing that embodies the most divinity. This is called divine wisdom.

Everything is as important
And indispensable
As everything else in God's creation.
Try to see the divine
In everything,
With everything
Plus for everything.

Have faith in yourself. You will have a new heart of assurance. Have faith in God. You will have a new life of accomplishment.

We have to be faithful both in the inner world and in the outer world. When we are faithful to our inner life, to our life of aspiration, or even when we are faithful to our outer activities, we feel that our divinity is blossoming petal by petal. When we go deep within, we see that there is only one person who is constantly and eternally faithful to us, and that is God. From time immemorial He has been faithful to us, faithful to His creation.

Because you have made faith
Your loving and illumining friend,
Your mind—your enemy number one—
Will no longer come to play with you.

SEPTEMBER

To make the fastest progress,
Be an absolutely cheerful
Hero-warrior
And take both victory and failure
As parallel experience-rivers
Leading to the sea
Of progress-delight.

It is your heart's inner volcano-intensity that sees and feels what your Inner Pilot is offering to you and inspires you to become inseparably one with Him.

If we follow the spiritual life, naturally we want to go to the Source, which is God. We want to be as divine and great as the Source. If our ultimate aim is to become divine or to become God Himself, then we have to be faithful to the world that we are living in. How do we have to be faithful? We have to attend at every moment to what we say and what we think. When a thought comes to us, if it is a divine thought, then we have to feel that it is a blessing that has entered into us. This blessing we have to offer to the world around us. If we can faithfully and silently offer this divine thought to the outer world, then we are fulfilling the God inside us.

A tamed mind
Can do anything.
It can even think
Of the Compassion-God
And the perfection-life.

Unless I consciously act from God's Heart, how can I soulfully and perfectly work for God's body, the creation?

When we perform any action, we have to feel in this action the Life of God, the Hands of God. When we are eating, we have to feel that the food is God. If we can see and feel God in everything and feel our constant oneness with God, then automatically we will be faithful to ourselves; and when we are faithful to ourselves, at that time we are bound to get what we are aspiring for.

Each soulful effort
And each resolute act
In the countless incidents
Of man's human life and divine life
Is proudly treasured
By the Absolute Supreme Himself.

Patience is divine strength.

Very often ordinary people do not know the meaning of patience. They feel that it is something feminine, a form of cowardice or a reluctant way of accepting the truth. They feel that because there is no other way left, we have to be patient. But if consciously we can be patient, then we are strengthening our inner will and lengthening the scope of our divine manifestation.

Be a heart of patience
And a life of dynamism.
God will love you more.

Be intensely inspired in all your being to sing only one song: self-improvement.

Each individual has to accept himself as he is: half ignorance and half knowledge. Unless we accept ourselves in totality, we can never reach the Goal. First, we have to accept darkness and light together. Then we have to give more importance, infinitely more importance, to the light in us. When we pay attention to light, light automatically spreads and darkness disappears. At that time we become totally what we are: God in the form of Self-manifestation.

I gave God what I have
And what I am:
My willingness.
God is now giving me
What He has and what He is:
His Fulness.

A life of peace is the result of our unconditional dedication to the Will of the Supreme. If we do not expect anything from the world, either good or bad, then we will have peace in our entire being.

Peace is man's greatest and highest blessing. Man thinks that he can get everything with prosperity; but if he is wanting in peace, then he is the worst possible beggar. We say "peace of mind," but actually we do not have peace in the mind. By staying in the mind, we can never have even a glimpse of peace. When we want peace, we have to go beyond the realm of the mind. How can we go beyond the mind? It is through our constant aspiration. That aspiration will enable us to collect the mind like a bundle and throw it into the sea of the heart. Then we will see that our mind, vital and physical—our whole existence—will be inundated with inner peace.

Every day try to increase
Your love of God.
Then peace will automatically unfold
In your unquiet mind.

Our tears to God are our greatest strength to bring down His adamantine Protection.

Prayer and meditation must go together. When we pray, we ask God to be responsible for us, and when we meditate, we consciously accept responsibility for God. When we pray, we offer God our responsibilities; we give our helpless, hopeless, useless existence to God. When we meditate, we become like lions; we become divine, devoted instruments of God. At that time we take upon ourselves God's responsibilities. One moment we give our existence to God because we are helpless; the next moment we ask God if we can do something for Him. Prayer takes us up to God, and then God fulfils us. Meditation brings God down to us, and then we fulfil God. The two should go together.

Your mind's climbing prayer
And your heart's glowing meditation
Can easily save you.
Your life need not remain
Forever paralysed
By helpless hopelessness.

A fountain of God-thought tells me that mine is not a weak and mortal birth.

Self-confidence comes into existence when we feel that there is some higher force that is constantly looking after us and guiding us. If we do not have that kind of feeling or belief, then we can have no abiding self-confidence. We have to cultivate faith in our Inner Pilot. Right now He is unknowable. If we pray and meditate, He becomes knowable. And if we continue along the spiritual path, He eventually becomes totally known. Self-confidence comes into existence when we offer our very existence to a higher force. If that higher force is right now only imaginary, no harm. If we have faith and if we surrender our existence to the higher force, then self-confidence is automatically achieved in our life of aspiration.

Do not allow your heart,
Like your mind,
To be cramped
In life's insecurity-cage.

Man is infinite, man is eternal, man is immortal. But how can we really feel that we are infinite, eternal, immortal? We can do so only on the strength of our selflessness and sacrifice to the Supreme in ourselves and in humanity.

Selflessness must be properly understood. If one feels that it is by virtue of sacrifice that he is becoming totally one with the rest of the world, then that is not selflessness. To be really selfless, one must already feel and realise his oneness with the entire creation. Otherwise, one will always be under the impression that he is doing something grand and great by offering himself and serving someone. But when oneness has already been achieved, felt and realised, at that time selflessness really acquires its meaning. The seeker knows that he is one with the universe, and with this oneness he is now playing his own part. At that time we cannot call selflessness something that we are offering. No, it is something that we are growing into. Each selfless act leads us to something greater, and that something greater also is ours.

Every day you should try
To set a personal record
In your unconditional self-giving.

My surrender-life tells me that God thinks of me all the time, whether I think of Him or not.

In the spiritual life when we surrender, we consciously surrender our lower life to our higher life. We surrender our lower life because we feel that our higher part is truly our very own. True surrender means the conscious acceptance by the finite of Infinity's will and vision. We have to surrender only to the one in whom we have perfect faith. We shall not surrender to others' thoughts or wills or commands or demands, even if they are superior to us in terms of age or position. No! We shall surrender only to Him in whom we have perfect faith, to the Reality, to the Inner Pilot from whom we will get our true fulfilment.

Surrender yourself
To the beauty of truth,
To the purity of light,
To the divinity of God's
Transcendental Height.

If your heart wants to land on the shore of delight, then your mind must say good-bye to the shore of thought.

Negative forces are those forces that tell you that you are hopeless and useless, that you cannot realise God and that it is useless to try. These are the forces that tell you not to pray and meditate because there is nothing in meditation. Positive forces make you feel that you are God's chosen child and that you have the possibility and potentiality of doing something significant for God and for your own divinity at every moment. If you remain in the heart, you will encounter very few negative forces, practically none. But if you live in the mind, the negative forces will often threaten you. It is almost impossible to conquer something with the mind. But with the heart, it is not only possible and practical, but inevitable that you will conquer all negative forces.

If you can live
Inside your silence-heart,
Then you can easily establish
Your satisfaction-delight
For humanity to enjoy.

If you want to know the ultimate Truth, then go beyond the human mind.

In the field of manifestation we have to be very, very careful with truth. Truth has to be spoken, but we have to know that God's Will is infinitely more important than the so-called utterance of truth. If we give the same importance to earthly mundane truth that we give to the eternal Truth, then we will be making a Himalayan mistake. If we speak truth just for the sake of truth, then we may create more disharmony, more frustration and more misery in life. Beyond the so-called earthly truth we have to see God's Vision, which is the ultimate Truth.

We realise the highest Truth
Only when we are fully prepared
To renounce the hungry cry
Of our desire-life

My soul represents God the Beauty in Heaven.

We can be sincere to our soul at every moment if we can make ourselves feel that the soul has to come first and foremost in our life. We have to make ourselves feel that the dream of the soul is the only thing that we need. The dream of the soul is our treasured breath and the manifestation of this dream is our only goal. If we have that kind of inner awareness, then at every moment we can be sincere to our soul's need and our soul's immortal reality.

You can be happy
Only when your mind accepts the fact
That somebody else has more wisdom-delight.
Who is that somebody?
None other than your own
Eternity's blue bird—your soul.

Conscience and intuition are the inner experiences of the soul that try to protect and perfect our outer life.

There are quite a few ways to develop one's intuition. The easiest way is to remain in the heart, become one with it, and cry and try to become what the soul has and what the soul is. You have to enter into the heart and cry for the soul, cry to have the soul and to become the soul. If you can remain in the heart and feel that the heart is a child who is all the time crying to become as good, as divine, as perfect as the mother or father, the soul, then automatically you develop the power of intuition.

*Do not read
Secret mind-thoughts,
But feel
Sacred heart-thoughts.*

Live every moment to please God. God lives every moment to illumine you.

If we want to recognise the message or voice of the Inner Pilot, then we have to know one thing: as soon as we get the message of the Inner Pilot, we will see that this message is giving us inner joy and inner satisfaction. Then, as soon as we carry out the message, the message will bear fruit in the form of success or failure. If we can take the result with the same cheerfulness, the same amount of inner strength, inner courage and equanimity whether it is success or failure, then we can be certain that the message to do this deed came from the soul.

One day you will believe
That God's way is not only a better way,
But also the only way
To transform your entire life.

Real divine practicality allows us to feel the divine motivation in all our actions and share the inner wealth from each action with others.

Before you act, try to feel that this action does not belong to you. And while acting, feel that you are not the doer, but someone else is acting in and through you. Then, when the result is out, you have to share it with others. Feel that it is not you who is acting, but rather the person who is inspiring you, who is acting in and through you. This person is none other than your Inner Pilot. If you can feel this, then you can have divine practicality in your life at every moment.

Why do you feel
That you are all alone?
There is someone
Who is thinking of you.
There is someone
Who is doing everything for you.

The most effective way to see the divine in others is to see at every second the divine in ourselves, in every cell of our body, in every breath that we consciously take in.

The reason that we are divine one moment and then become undivine the next moment is that we separate one second from the next. But this we should not do. If this moment we feel that we are divine, or that someone else is divine, then we should not wait for the next moment to bring another type of experience. We should try to lengthen this experience rather than have another experience. We have to think of this experience as a train, and allow the train to go from one station to another station without stopping at any place. The experience should go from one second to another in a continuous movement.

Keep your division-mind.
Nobody wants it!
Keep your oneness-heart.
Everybody needs it!

You cannot unconditionally love God and vehemently dislike man at the same time.

There is also another way to see the divinity in others and that is to always think of the Source. There is something in you that wants you to see divinity in others. If you try to trace that thing, you will see that it is not the physical, the vital or the mind. The physical in you cries only to sleep for a few more hours. The vital in you wants only to dominate the world and lord it over others. The mind wants to find fault with the rest of the world. But something inside the physical, the vital and the mind is inspiring you to see the divine inside others. If you search for the thing that is inspiring you, you will find that it is the inner cry coming from your soul. This inner cry constantly wants satisfaction, and satisfaction comes only in devotion, only in oneness, only in seeing the divine in yourself and others and becoming devotedly and unreservedly one with it.

The mind has only one road:
Division-road.
The heart has many roads:
Soulfulness-road,
Fruitfulness-road
And oneness-road.

Do not ask mankind for its opinion once you have heard God's life-transformation Command.

There is someone who will follow you faithfully through Eternity like a dog, and that is the Supreme. Pay attention only to the Supreme. He will go wherever you go, whether it be Heaven or hell. This moment He tells you, "I am right ahead of you; just follow Me. Do not worry. I shall be with you wherever you go." The next moment He will say, "Go ahead, I am right behind you. I will follow him who is ready to follow Me." The Supreme will always follow you, no matter where you go, but no human being will do this. No human being is going to follow you to the end of your life, not to speak of following you for Eternity. And the Supreme will gladly and cheerfully allow you to follow Him. So what is the use of following human beings or allowing them to follow you? If you have that kind of feeling for the Supreme, if you are devoted only to Him, then your human attachment will go away. And when human attachment goes away, devotion to the Supreme takes birth, grows, develops and reaches perfection.

If you can live
In your soulful experience,
Then you and God
Will have a common name:
Satisfaction.

Constant expectation in one's own way is an infallible way of losing one's present joy.

We are crying and crying for happiness in the form of expectation. But no matter what we seek, the results will be limited. We have to know that there is somebody with infinite capacity who is eager and anxious to share with us His capacity. Let us be wise; let us give Him the chance. Let us allow His expectation to be fulfilled in us. Let His expectation grow in and through us. Let our human expectation be conquered by the divine expectation of the Supreme, the Eternal Pilot. Let us surrender our human expectation to the Supreme's expectation. When we surrender to the unlimited light, we become really unlimited. If we take this attitude, we act like divine children, children of light, children of wisdom. At that time, our expectation is conquered by His expectation, which is unlimited. This way only, through surrender, can we conquer our human expectation.

O my Lord Supreme,
Do show me the way to unload
My load of constant expectation.
Absolutely unbearable
Is my expectation-load!

Each person is fallible, yet each person will eventually become God's perfect representative on earth.

In this world, we notice that one thing alternates with another. Day alternates with night, fear alternates with courage, doubt alternates with faith, self-love alternates with God-love. But when we become unconditionally surrendered seekers of God, our oneness with God never alternates.

If you are a true God-lover,
Then it is quite possible
For you to foresee
That in the battle between
Aspiration-heart and suspicion-mind,
Aspiration-heart will eventually win.

You can have perfect peace only when you can halt your mind's journey at God's Forgiveness-Feet.

When you have divine peace, realisation cannot help knocking at your heart's door. The lotus of realisation will start blooming in your heart, petal by petal. To realise God, temples, churches and synagogues are not obligatory. Neither is the tapestry of scriptures and sermons required. What is imperative is meditation. Meditation will make you realise God the Infinite within your soul, heart, mind and body.

Meditation, like an angel, came
To enlighten his mind,
To liberate his heart,
To immortalise his life.

Let us all be truly spiritual. Let us realise God through our constant communion with Him.

God is your own highest, most illumined, most perfect part. You have two parts: one is higher, one is lower. Most of the time you stay in the lower part. When you become fully aware of your higher part and your lower part is totally transformed and unified with your highest part, at that time you are none other than God. Although it is not yet recognised or revealed, your own highest, most developed, most perfect and illumined part is God.

My heart-garden
Is absolutely the best place
For me to meditate
For my self-discovery.

God hides His Face because He enjoys the game: hide-and-seek.

Everybody has to define God in his own way. God is above and beyond all description. You may say God is an infinite expanse of consciousness. The one who is sitting beside you may say, "No, God is infinite light," and a third may say, "God is all power." A fourth person may say, "God is personal. He is like a human being: He has two hands, two eyes, a nose and so forth." Each person will define God in his own way. My definition is this: God is man yet to be fully manifested, and man is God yet to be fully realised. We are all human beings, but at the same time we are God.

The moment you know
Who you really are,
All secrets of the world
Will be an open book to you.

God-discovery is nothing other than a matter of not giving up the game.

In the beginning everybody experiences ups and downs in the spiritual life. When a child is learning to walk, in the beginning he stumbles and falls again and again and again. But after a while he learns to walk properly and finally to run. Eventually he can run as fast as his capacity will allow. But a small child cannot expect to run as fast as his father does, because his father has much more capacity. When you are up, you have to feel that you are getting a glimpse of your eventual capacity. When you are down, you should simply feel that this is only a temporary incapacity. Just because you see that those who are more advanced than you in the spiritual life are running, you must not be discouraged. Once upon a time they also stumbled.

Be brave within and without!
Do not allow the tyranny
Of past memories
To destroy your heart's hope-bridge,
Which will carry you
To the other shore,
The shore of light and delight.

My meditation is my birthless and deathless joy.

When life is not giving you joy but you feel that you want joy, that means you are hungry. In the spiritual life, when you are hungry, you will eat spiritual food. When you are not hungry, you will not eat. For fifteen or twenty years, let us say, you did not sincerely and intensely care for the spiritual life. Since you did not meditate intensely for so many years, if you jump all at once into the sea of spirituality you will not be able to swim. You cannot change your nature overnight. It has to be done slowly, steadily, gradually. First move around in the water; then gradually you will learn how to swim. Then there will come a time when you will be able to swim well. But since you have inner hunger, that means you are ready to start swimming.

If a sincere seeker
Does not pray and meditate regularly,
There comes a time
When the throbs of his inner pain
Pulse in very rapid succession
In the depths of his soulful heart.

Spirituality is not impatience.

The seeker has to know that we cannot realise the transcendental Truth overnight. There is no short-cut. It takes time and it demands constant effort. The seeker walks along Eternity's Road. Each time he reaches his destination, he sees that that destination becomes the starting point for a higher destination.

> *Who says*
> *There is nothing to sacrifice?*
> *Our wild impatience*
> *Has to be sacrificed*
> *Every day,*
> *Every hour,*
> *Every minute,*
> *Every second.*

The life of possession constantly makes us think only of success in life.

In order to arrive at the door of success, many times we adopt foul means. Even if we do not adopt foul means, we are always in the world of competition. By competing with others, even by defeating others, the joy and satisfaction that we get cannot last. When we feel that we have become something on the strength of our success, our sincerity tells us that there is someone superior to us. Somebody becomes a great poet, a great athlete, a great singer, and he is bloated with pride. But when he looks around, in the twinkling of an eye he sees that there is somebody who writes far better than he does, somebody who plays sports or sings far better than he. In every walk of life he sees somebody better than himself. So success finally becomes frustration, and frustration is bound to be followed by destruction.

The heart of progress-oneness
Satisfies both God and man.
The mind of success-prowess
Satisfies only man.

Meditation means the language of our inner life and the language of God. It is through meditation that we can commune with God. It is through meditation that we can see God face to face.

Each person has to have a meditation of his own. He has to get it from the inmost recesses of his heart or from a spiritual teacher. If you want to launch into the inner life of aspiration, the life of the soul, then you will need a teacher who can teach you to concentrate, meditate and contemplate. Until you get a teacher, you may not be sure what message your inner voice is giving you. You can start by reading scriptures and spiritual books. These books will instruct you how to discipline your life to some extent. But if you want to go to the end of the road and reach your inner Goal, then you need true meditation.

Read spiritual books
With your heart's aspiration;
You will understand everything.
Read them with your mind's suspicion;
You will understand nothing.

Poor human mind! What else does it know except thought-mud-pleasure?

During meditation our heart gets the real realisation of Truth. After we stop meditating, our mind immediately tells us something else. It says, "No, this message cannot be right." The mind has its own realisation, which it thinks is better and more profitable than the realisation of the heart. But it may be that the realisation which seems to be the less profitable of the two is actually the higher realisation.

Give to God what you have:
Your mind's slow train to hell.
God will give you what He has:
His Heart's fast Boat to Heaven.

Be wise! Ask your heart to feel, and do not ask your mind to understand.

The heart always offers the same message. When we sit down to meditate in the morning, it gives one message. In the evening when we meditate, we will again get the same message from the heart. But in the case of the mind, one moment it says one thing, and the next moment it says something else. One moment the mind will say, "He is a good man. Last night he appreciated me in front of other people." But the next moment our mind remembers the past, even though the past is now irrelevant. Then it says, "He is a rascal. He lied to me twenty years ago." So let us always listen to the dictates of the heart.

Think of your heart all the time.
Sooner or later
Your mind will not mind
Following your heart.

OCTOBER

Three signs of progress:
To do something better
Than you have previously done it,
To maintain your standard,
To have a cheerful heart
Even if your standard goes down.

There shall come a time when each and every human being will enjoy the bright burst of oneness-delight.

We are now experiencing the finite. Unfortunately, we have not yet experienced the Infinite, the Immortal and the Eternal. Just because we have not yet felt the Infinite, we feel that the opposite—the finite—is hell. But we have to know that the bondage that we are experiencing every day is only a passing phase. It is like an overcast day. For a few hours the sun does not shine, but finally the sun comes out. Each individual has an inner sun. This inner sun is now covered by fear, doubt, worries, anxiety, imperfections and limitations. But a day will come when we will be able to remove these clouds, and then the inner sun will shine brightly.

Do you want to shine?
You can easily shine
Like the sun
In your self-offering
To God in man.

Even an iota of expectation can destroy your Himalayan-high ecstasy.

When we meditate, we must not expect anything from our meditation. God is meditating in and through us. The very fact that we want to meditate should please us. Millions of people are not meditating; they are wallowing in the pleasures of ignorance. How is it that out of millions and billions of people, we are ready to meditate? God has chosen us. The very fact that we are meditating means that we have been blessed by God. Here we have to know that He who has given us the capacity to meditate will also give us the result. But there is something called God's choice Hour. Just because we have started meditating, we cannot expect peace, light and bliss overnight.

God is ready to spring a surprise
Every day in my aspiration-life
If I renounce my expectation-mind
Once and for all.

A feeble prayer brings down God's omnipotent Grace. Such is the magnanimity of God's Compassion.

We have to feel that we are divine farmers. We cultivate the land and sow the seed. Then we have to wait for rain, for the divine Grace. A farmer does not get a bumper crop in a day. Similarly, a spiritual seeker will not get the bumper crop of God-realisation in a single day. If he wants to do this, then he is pushing or pulling beyond the capacity of his receptivity. He will naturally be frustrated and this frustration he will call hell. He must wait for God's choice Hour and remain satisfied with the idea that God will give him the capacity to meditate at His choice Hour. Patience is necessary. God has given us the capacity to meditate, so we should be grateful that He has chosen us right now. If we pull, if we push, then frustration will appear; and in frustration we will feel hell. We will doubt our own spiritual capacity and God's existence. So if we meditate for God's sake and not for our own sake, then we will never have doubt or the feeling of hell.

To triumph over our earthly sorrows
What we need
Is the power of our own faith
And the Hour of God's choice.

God's Grace-Kingdom is my only home. The rest of the world is nothing but a stopping place.

God's Grace is always there, but how many people utilise it? God's Grace is like the rays of the sun. The sun is always there, but what do we do? We get up late. Instead of getting up at five-thirty or six o'clock, we get up at eight or nine o'clock. Then we do not get the blessing of the morning sun. And when we do get up, we keep the doors and windows all shut and do not allow the sunlight to enter into our room. In the spiritual life also, God's Grace is constantly descending, but we are not allowing the Grace to enter into our system. We have kept barriers between God's Grace and our own ignorance. Only if we keep our heart's door wide open can God's Light enter into our existence.

If you have the capacity
To create the clouds of trouble,
Then God has the capacity
To create the sun of Grace.
For whom, if not for you,
For you alone?

He is enjoying a feast with his heart's ascending sun and his Lord's descending Grace.

God's Grace is constantly descending; this is absolutely true. We have to empty our inner vessel every day and fill the vessel with God's Peace, Light and Bliss. We have to feel that God's Light is there all the time and is more than willing to illumine us. Then only will we be able to utilise God's Grace. Again, if we miss God's Grace, we should not be doomed to disappointment. Today we have not allowed the sunlight to enter into our room, but tomorrow again the sun will be there. If today we have not allowed God's Grace to enter into us due to our ignorance, no harm. Tomorrow we will definitely be prepared for God's Light to enter into us.

Unless you become today
God's Satisfaction-Grace,
How will you see tomorrow
God's Perfection-Face?

No end to sadness for him who mechanically thinks and thinks. No end to joy for him who prayerfully meditates and meditates.

If one follows the spiritual path, then one has to meditate at least once a day. This is obligatory. It is better to meditate at least three times a day, but if it is not possible to feed your soul three times, then please feed it at least once. Feel that the soul is a little child, a divine child. If you do not feed the soul, then it will starve, and your divine manifestation will be delayed.

Before I meditate,
God places His Compassion-Drink before me
And asks me to help myself.
After I have meditated,
God places His Satisfaction-Feast before me
And asks me to help myself.

To arrive at the core of everything, what you need is an ardent submissiveness to Eternity's infinite Source.

The spiritual aspirant should always bear in mind that he is of God and he is for God. Right now he may be a budding seeker, he may be a beginner; so for him God cannot be or need not be always a living God. Sometimes the aspirant will only be able to imagine God, and sometimes, in spite of his outer efforts, he may not feel the presence of God in himself. Sometimes he may even forget the existence of God. But he has to bear in mind that he has a Source and that Source is light, boundless light, infinite light. He has been wallowing in the pleasures of ignorance for many years, but he has to feel that his Source is not ignorance; his Source is light and delight. He is for that Source and he is making a conscious effort to return to his Source. While returning, he is manifesting God-delight here on earth. Although he is in ignorance to some degree, he is always for God-life and he is always for God-light. If he can remember this, then he will feel a constant sense of satisfaction in his life. He will feel light, more light, abundant light, infinite light in his outer and inner life.

When I feel that I am of God,
I clearly see
That God is my only lamp.
When I feel that I am for God,
I clearly see
That God's Light is in me.

What is the mind, if not a conscious fantasy of ridiculous and superfluous demands?

The mind needs a superior power to keep it quiet. This superior power is the power of the soul. We have to bring to the fore the light of the soul, which has unlimited power. In the outer world, when somebody is superior in strength or power, he tries to punish the inferior. But in the spiritual world, the light of the soul will not torture or punish the mind. On the contrary, it will act like a most affectionate mother who feels that the imperfections of her child are her own imperfections. The heart will feel the obscurity, impurity and darkness of the mind as its own imperfections and, at the same time, the heart will be in a position to offer its light to the mind. In pin-drop silence it will try to transform the nature of the mind.

The beginning of perfection
Dawns
When the seeker puts an end
To his critical mind.

I bow to the Light that never dims.

Right now our goal is purest light. In this case, our work is to cry inwardly. We have to inwardly cry like a child for inseparable oneness with the Supreme. The child cries for what it wants, and the mother always comes. No matter where she is, she comes to offer the child whatever it wants. Similarly, when we cry in the inmost recesses of our heart, our request is granted. But everything depends on the sincerity of our inner cry. If our cry is sincere, God is bound to grant it. If we cry inwardly for spiritual things—for peace, light and bliss—then we are bound to achieve these divine qualities.

I do not need miracles, please.
I do not even want
To see miracles, please.
I need and expect only
A crying heart and a smiling life.

**Your new-made friendship with your con-
science-life will save you, perfect you and
finally illumine you.**

An advanced seeker constantly listens to his conscience. His conscience is his code of life. His
conscience is his art. His conscience is his religion. When he does something good, he feels
that he is following his code of life. When he does
something bad, he feels that he has swerved from
the path of truth and that he is no longer faithful
to his code of life, his art, his religion.

My accusing conscience,
I love you because you care for me,
My perfection.
My illumining conscience,
I love you because you care
For the supreme satisfaction
Of my Beloved Supreme
Within me.

Desire binds us; aspiration liberates us.

When we desire, we try to increase our capacities in order to challenge others, in order to defeat others, in order to lord it over others, and in order to make the world feel that we are a few inches—if not a few miles—ahead of it. When we aspire, we cry not only for our own perfection, but also for others' perfection. Aspiration plays the role of oneness, which is nothing other than perfection itself. When we remain in the ordinary world, the unaspiring world, the desire-world, we try to please and satisfy only ourselves. But when we are in the aspiration-world, we try to please God. If we can please God on the strength of our heart's inner cry, then we will see and feel inside us God's Love, Concern, Light and Peace—all that God has and is.

Peace-meditation
Can not only annihilate
Your mind's restlessness
But also liberate your life
From desire-night.

It is your heart's orphan-cries that will help you reach the heights of God's Beauty supreme.

When we cry inwardly, we have to feel a sincere need for God. When we have that inner need, then God, out of His infinite Bounty, will come and grant us the things that we need. If we have a sincere, genuine inner cry, then all our problems will be solved. But if we do not have that sincere inner cry, then no matter how many years we live on earth, we will not find satisfaction, because true satisfaction means the perfection of our nature, the perfection of our life.

To be closer to God
I need two things:
A heart that knows
How to cry sleeplessly
And a mind that believes
In self-illumination.

If something is true, you will feel it within the very depths of your heart.

You sow a seed. After a few months it germinates. In a year it grows into a sapling, and eventually it grows into a huge banyan tree. When you begin to take an interest in the spiritual life, you have only sown the seed. You may not see the results immediately. It takes time. You have to start with faith—sincere, genuine, sublime faith. You have to pray and meditate before you will feel your own divinity. If you cannot feel your inner divinity right now, do not be sad or upset. It takes time. Pray and meditate sincerely and through your faith, your real divinity will one day loom large. If you do not have higher experiences or realisations as soon as you enter into the spiritual life, do not give up. Right now if you do not feel inside the very depths of your heart something divine, illumining, fulfilling and perfect, no harm. It takes time to acquire a free access to the inner world. But once you have a free access to the inner world, you will see that it is flooded with light and delight.

For me there is only one friend,
And that friend is
My heart's ever-blossoming faith.
I need no second friend.

Arguments often prefer religion to truth.

There are two kinds of religions: false religions and true religions. A false religion wants to change the face of the world by any means, even by foul means—by hook or by crook. A true religion wants only to love soulfully the heart of the world. A false religion will try to exercise its Himalayan supremacy over other religions. A true religion will only sympathise with other religions. It wants to experience its oneness-ecstasy with all religions, founded upon its own soulful cry. It wants to become inseparably one with all religions by virtue of its tolerance, patience, kindness and forgiveness. Again, a true religion knows perfectly well that it is the Supreme Pilot Himself who is loving and piloting each religion, and at the same time forgiving the shortcomings that each religion unfortunately embodies.

The essence of religion:
Fear God and obey God.
The quintessence of spirituality:
Love God and become another God.

It takes a heroic heart to say no to the desire-world.

Right now we are living the life of desire. But even when our desires are fulfilled, we are usually not satisfied at all. We want something desperately in the desire-life, but when we get that very thing, immediately we are dissatisfied. It has happened in our lives many, many times. While we are crying for some particular thing, we never care that somebody else already has it. But when we get what we wanted, we look around and see that thousands of other people also have it, and perhaps they have more of it than we do. They have the same thing in abundant measure, whereas we have only a limited amount. So we are dissatisfied. No matter how much we have of something in the desire-life, it is never enough for us.

In my desire-life
What I actually need
Is an endless "No!"

You want to fulfil your desires? Then you have to do it all at your own risk.

The fulfilment of desire is not the answer. What we have to do is try to minimise our desires and totally enter into the life of aspiration. If we can minimise our desires, then along with our desires, our destructive thoughts and tendencies will also decrease. Aspiration is a flame. This flame illumines and purifies everything that is uncomely and undivine within us, so that real satisfaction can be ours.

Absolute honesty
Is absolutely needed
To transform your desire-night
Into aspiration-day.

Aspiration and failure do not know each other.

If we aspire regularly, soulfully and sincerely, then self-destructive thoughts will not assail our mind, and self-destructive actions will not embrace our life. We have to walk along the positive path of aspiration which will carry us high, higher, highest. The higher we go, the more aspiration-flames we will see in our obscure life, and our obscure, impure, destructive thoughts will be illumined. A room can remain dark for days, months and years, but as soon as we turn on the light switch, the room is all illumined. Then it is easy for us to clean and purify the room. Similarly, if we do not aspire, if we do not pray and meditate, then our mind-room remains dark. But the moment we aspire, the moment we turn on the light with our inner cry, it becomes easy for us to transform our life completely.

Your life's ultimate victory
Depends on the surrender
Of your heart's
Aspiration-flames.

Every day must come to you as a new hope, a new promise, a new aspiration, a new energy, a new thrill and a new delight.

If you think that tomorrow will be another day like those which you have already seen, then you will make no progress. You have to feel that tomorrow will be something absolutely new that you are going to create in your life. Every day you have to energise yourself to such an extent that you feel new hope and new aspiration. If on a particular day there is no hope, then on that day you are dead. If on a particular day there is no promise, then you are worse than dead. If you want to live on earth, then you must have hope. Hope is not a mental hallucination. Far from it. Hope is a vast field. And if there is promise, then you can feel that you have sown the seed, the promise-seed.

I have only one home,
And that is my hope-home.
When I abandon this home
I have nowhere to go.
I am all alone
In misery's land.

Each sacred hope is a blessingful gift from Heaven's heart.

It is only with newness, newness at every moment in life, that you can succeed and transcend yourself. If you always have the hope of newness in thought and in action, then only can you transcend. What you have is good, but it is not enough. You need something more. You should feel that you cannot manifest the Supreme unless you become infinite like Him. You need more, but not for your own personal fulfilment or aggrandisement. Without infinite peace and infinite light, how are you going to manifest the infinite Supreme? Therefore, you have to treasure hope and promise at every moment. It is with hope and promise that you can think of Infinity, and it is only with Infinity that you can fulfil the message of Infinity.

If you do not have new hope,
New aspiration and new dedication
Every day,
Then where is your true awakening?

Optimism is the secret of self-reliance. Self-reliance is the secret of dynamic power. Dynamic power is the secret of immediate success.

Our human difficulty is that we do not take anything seriously. We hope for name and fame, but if we see that we must climb up a tall tree in order to get what we want, then we lose interest. In the spiritual life also we want God, but before we realise God, we have to do a few things. If we feel inwardly the value of God-realisation in our life, then the so-called hardship that we go through is nothing. If we value the goal, then we are bound to walk along the path. The road is long and arduous, but if we constantly keep the goal in our view and walk along the road, then we will reach our destination. If we really value the goal and cry for the goal, then there will always be some way for us to reach the goal.

*Your life
Is God's responsibility
If you care for
The divinity within you only.*

Fear. What is it? When we follow the spiritual life, we come to realise sooner than at once that fear is a real enemy. What does it do? It buys our coffin long before we are destined to die.

Meditation is the only way to overcome fear. There is no other way. Why does meditation help us to overcome our fear? In meditation we identify ourselves with the Vast, with the Absolute. When we are afraid of someone or something, it is because we do not feel that particular person or thing is a part of us. When we have established conscious oneness with the Absolute, with the infinite Vast, then everything included there is part of us. And how can we be afraid of ourselves?

Every day the fear-world
Has fearful messages for you.
But you are under no obligation
To listen to the messages
Of the fear-world.

Real inner joy we get only when our aspiration is genuine and sincere. When we have inner joy, we see and feel that we are consciously sitting and growing in the lap of God.

If anybody wants to know whether his aspiration is genuine and whether he is really marching toward the Goal or not, then I wish to ask that person to observe his mind and heart. If in his mind he feels inner joy and peace and if his heart is flooded with joy and delight, not pleasure, then his aspiration is true and genuine. At that time the aspirant will know that he is not deceiving himself.

You can climb fast, very fast,
The progress-tree
If you give what you have:
Inspiration-drops
And aspiration-flames.

In pursuing peace of mind, the first step is to sincerely feel that no individual is indispensable.

An individual may have a few good qualities, but that does not mean that he or she is indispensable. The same good qualities others may have. The more we give importance to ourselves or others, the more we weaken our own capacity. Only God is indispensable. We have to give all importance to the Source, to the Divine within us, to the Supreme within us. We have to feel that we are able to serve others and they are able to serve us precisely because the Supreme has given us certain qualities. These qualities have a true possessor, and the possessor is the Supreme. If we can consciously and continuously make ourselves feel that He alone is indispensable, then we can have peace of mind.

Only a fool
Thinks that he is independent.
Only a fool
Feels that he is indispensable.

I want to live forever where I am living now: on the summit of my hope-mountain.

When we are sincere, we feel that God loves us. When we pray, we feel that God belongs to us. When we meditate, we feel that we are of God. Our sincerity leads us along the right path. Our prayer accelerates our speed. Our meditation brings the goal nearer to us.

> *You must daily pray and meditate.*
> *A simple thing like that*
> *Will bring God*
> *The infinite Compassion and Satisfaction*
> *To you.*

It is absolutely necessary to prevent oneself from giving off impure vital love. Otherwise, one will constantly have to wrestle with the gigantic forces of ignorance.

One has to use love not to bind or possess the world, but to free and widen one's own consciousness and the consciousness of the world. One must not try to substitute the heart's pure love for the impure vital love. What one must do is to bring the heart's purifying and transforming love into the impure vital. The vital, as such, is not bad at all. When the vital is controlled, purified and transformed, it becomes a most significant instrument of God.

Only when our dynamic vital
Challenges the wild emotional vital
Can our soul erase
Our deplorable past mistakes.
Only then, in our life of aspiration,
Shall we feel continuous success
And continuous progress.

The reasoning mind must be transformed into a dedicated instrument of the Supreme.

The reasoning mind is really an obstacle for an aspirant. Using the mind becomes a limitation because the mind cannot grasp the Infinite. If we live in the mind, we will constantly try to circumscribe the Truth; we will never be able to see the Truth in its proper form. Only if we live in the soul will we be able to embrace the Truth as a whole. Beyond the boundaries of the reasoning mind are Truth, Reality and Infinity. Reason has very limited light, whereas what we want and need is infinite light. When infinite light dawns, reason is broken into pieces.

If you are ready
To live outside the reason-fort,
Then God will grant you
His own Perfection-Satisfaction-Home.

Your soul needs absolute fulfilment. It wants to achieve this absolute fulfilment not in Heaven, but here on earth.

If you live in the body, you will be too weak to prevent anything. If you live in the vital, you will be too authoritarian to allow anything. If you live in the mind, you will be too indifferent to love anything. If you live in the heart, you will be too indulgent to control anything. Live in the soul; God will say, do and become everything for you.

My all-devouring vital tells me
That I can do whatever I want.
My God-loving heart tells me
That I have nothing to do,
For my Lord has already done
Everything for me,
And He will do the same always.

Your soul is the self-effulgent messenger of God within you. It knows no birth, no decay, no death. It is eternal. It is immortal.

Your soul is unique. God wants to manifest and fulfil Himself within you in an unprecedented way. God has a particular divine mission to fulfil only through your soul. To fulfil this particular mission of His, He will utilise your soul and no other soul as His chosen instrument. Do you want your life to be of service to God so that you can fulfil His mission? If so, then here and now give the soul back its throne. You have driven the soul away and placed the ego on its throne. Do cordially welcome the soul and unite yourself with it. At that time, fear leaves you, ignorance leaves you and finally, death leaves you. Eternity welcomes you, Infinity welcomes you and finally, Immortality welcomes you.

Remember what you said to God in Heaven
Before you left for earth.
Your constant remembrance
Will be transformed into a perfect performance.

Permanent happiness you wanted. Unending sorrow you have got. Why? Because you love your earth-reality in your own way and not in God's own way.

Why do we experience suffering? In this world we are always consciously or unconsciously making mistakes. When we consciously make mistakes, we are quite aware of it. But unfortunately, we do not see the millions of things that we are doing wrong unconsciously. These unconscious mistakes manifest themselves in the physical world and the results come to us as suffering. If people who repeatedly make mistakes have sincere aspiration and want to know why they are suffering, then the soul's light comes to the fore and tells them. If we are spiritual people, consciously we will not do anything wrong, but unconsciously we may do many things wrong. We can prevent unconscious mistakes only through our aspiration, prayer and meditation. If we aspire, then God's Grace and Compassion protect us.

Do not be afraid of the piercing dart
Of today's sorrow,
For tomorrow will dawn
With its ecstasy-hours
Of light and delight.

Do not think of human grief. Think only of your eagerness to transform it into divinity's divine joy-flames.

God does not want suffering for human beings. He is the Father of Love. When we go to our Father, we do not have to cut off our arms or our legs. We will go with all our love because He is waiting for us with His Love. If we say that we have to suffer in order to go to our Father, that is stupidity. God, our Father, does not want our suffering. But when suffering does come, we have to feel that even in this suffering there is a divine intention. If we really aspire, suffering itself will give us a real experience which will make us feel that we are nearer to our goal. We should never find fault with God because of our suffering. It is we who have invited suffering through our conscious or unconscious mistakes. When suffering comes to us, we have to pray to God to free us from this suffering. We have to know that suffering is not our goal; our goal is delight.

He has departed
From his earthly pain
Not by leaving the body,
But by becoming inseparably one
With his soul-sea's
Ecstasy-waves.

A soulful heart questions the authenticity of the mind.

If the mind is searching and crying, it can help raise the level of consciousness. But the mind can never help us maintain a high level of consciousness. Only the light of the soul has the capacity to do that. The soul has given this capacity to the heart and the heart can do it on behalf of the soul. If our soul helps us, then our consciousness remains perfect. But if the help comes from the heart which is not yet fully illumined, then our consciousness does not remain on the same high level. Nevertheless, the heart has far more capacity than the mind to help us maintain a high level of consciousness.

Your cloud-eclipsed mind
Will invariably fail you.
Your starlit heart
Will not only fulfil you
But also immortalise you.

NOVEMBER

When a true God-lover
Cannot decide what to do
In his outer life,
God, out of His infinite Bounty,
Takes it as His bounden Duty
To help that person choose
The right thing to do.

Do you want to make progress? If so, then take each problem not as a challenging, but as an encouraging friend of yours, who is helping you to arrive at your ultimate destination.

Problems do not indicate man's incapacity. Problems do not indicate man's inadequacy. Problems do not indicate man's insufficiency. Problems indicate man's conscious need for self-transcendence in the inner world, and his conscious need for self-perfection in the outer world.

Each difficulty
Is a hard examination:
So says my truth-fearing mind.
Each difficulty
Is an increased strength:
So says my God-loving heart.

If our consciousness is low, immediately we can stop our bad thoughts with our will-power.

If we have good thoughts, with our will-power we can strengthen them. Will-power can easily destroy our bad thoughts and negate the wrong forces in us. And with will-power also we can increase the power of our good thoughts and increase our good qualities. So if we use our will-power properly, we can perform miracle after miracle in our lives. And even if we do not, through our prayer and meditation, develop our will-power, still with our sincere aspiration and sincere inner cry we can also do these things. So pray and meditate, and develop your aspiration and gratitude. Then you will really see the difference in your life.

The will that makes
A purity-flooded saint
Will not remain far away
If you desperately and sleeplessly
Cry for it.

From today on I shall try to have a new type of success. My conscious surrender to the Will of my Beloved Supreme will be my only success.

God is for those who are absolutely sincere and absolutely determined to become His choice instruments. If you are absolutely determined to become His choice instrument, then He will inspire you, help you and guide you to the Highest. You have to decide what you actually want. The Highest, the Deepest, the Ultimate and the Absolute are not mere words. They are realities, absolute realities, that can be achieved only by pleasing God in God's own way.

My dear Lord,
I wish to be led
Every day.
My sweet Lord,
I wish to be led
In every way.
My beloved Lord,
I wish to be led
All the way.

Forgiveness of teeming sins is good. Illumination of teeming sins is better. Not to resort at any time to sin is by far the best.

The Supreme illumines the past by forgiveness. Real forgiveness means forgetfulness, conscious forgetfulness. If somebody really forgives you for something that you did, then he will not keep the memory even in his inner vision. But if he does not forgive you, he keeps it in front of his inner vision. Illumination is necessary because of darkness. Mistakes are darkness. So the Supreme illumines our mistakes through forgiveness.

God's Forgiveness finds me
No matter where I am.
God's Compassion takes me
Where I ought to go.

If you know how to disobey, then God also knows how to forgive.

On rare occasions we see imperfections in ourselves, but we always see imperfections in others. When we discover that we are imperfect or have done something wrong, what do we do? We forgive ourselves immediately, or we ignore the fact that we have done something wrong, or we decide to turn over a new leaf and never do it again. We do all these things in order to get satisfaction. If others do something wrong, if we do not forgive them, if we harbour undivine thoughts against them or want to punish them, we will never find true satisfaction. In order to satisfy ourselves, our reality, we must forgive others too. Forgiveness is illumination. We have to feel that by forgiving others we are illumining ourselves, our own enlarged, expanded self.

I always pray to God for forgiveness
When I do something wrong.
If God forgives me,
Then who can punish me?

If we can think of ourselves as divine instruments, we can feel that God is having an experience in and through us.

In God's dictionary there is no such word as "failure." What we see in His dictionary is "experience." Failure is an experience. Success is an experience. We can and we should accept them with the same joy. When God does something on the outer plane, because of our own preconceived ideas, we call one result success and one result failure. But God does not use His Mind. God manifests an experience which the human being needs to go through. He gives whatever experience is necessary to have. But human beings have preconceived ideas about what success is. They depend on outer results. Failure immediately ruins all their inspiration, and success carries them up to the skies. In God's case, it is all experience. When He starts, does and ends, He is only having a series of experiences.

Lord Supreme,
Make me a hallowed instrument,
A flute,
So that You can play on me
With Your all-illumining,
All-liberating
And all-immortalising
Delight.

My life is forgiven by God. Therefore, my heart feels obliged to forgive the world around me.

If we do not forgive, what happens? We place a heavy load on our shoulders. If I have done something wrong and I do not try to forgive myself or illumine myself, I will harbour the idea that I have made a mistake. And each time I think of my wrong action, I will only add to my heavy load of guilt. Similarly, if others have done me an act of injustice, the more I think of this, the heavier becomes my load of anger and resentment. Now, I have to run towards my goal. If I place something heavy on my shoulders, how am I going to run? I will see that others are all running very fast, while I can hardly walk.

What kind of goodness is it
If you keep it always on guard?
What kind of forgiveness is it
If you keep it always unused?

Character gives the key to open the most beautiful doors of life: peace of mind and delight.

Every day, early in the morning, stand in front of the mirror. If you dare to stand in front of the mirror, then you can easily stand in front of the whole world. When you stand in front of the mirror, if you see an undivine face looking back at you, then rest assured that the whole world is undivine. But if you are getting joy from your face, if it is pure and divine, then rest assured that the world is also pure and divine. According to the way you see yourself, the rest of the world will present itself to you.

Smile sleeplessly
And give unconditionally
So that with every heartbeat of yours
You can be worthy
Of God's transcendental Pride.

A confidence-heart and an assurance-mind are undoubtedly two immortal boons from above to humanity.

Confidence is of paramount importance. If we have confidence in ourselves and in God, then definitely we can make fast progress. If we have confidence only in God and not in ourselves, we will not be able to go very fast. If we have confidence only in ourselves and not in God, then we will not be able to make much progress either. We have to feel our confidence in God and God's Confidence in us. Our confidence in God we shall feel on the strength of our own dedication, and God's Confidence in us we can feel in and through the Compassion-Light which He bestows upon us constantly and unconditionally.

If you wage war
Against your unbelief,
God will immediately grant you
His own Confidence-Light.

Spirituality is man's conscious longing for God.

Spirituality tells us that God, who is unknowable today, will tomorrow become knowable and the day after will become totally known. We must need God for God's sake. God can fulfil us in our own way, but it is we who will not be truly fulfilled when God satisfies us in our own way. Our crying heart, our aspiring heart, our illumining heart will never be satisfied unless and until it pleases God in God's own way. Therefore, our God-realisation is for God's sake.

If God is what you want,
Then He can never come second.
He will always come first.
He will come
As your Confidant.
He will come
As your Advisor Supreme.
He will come
As your only Friend.

You want to race against death. I tell you, you will succeed. Just carry one thing with you: a tiny gratitude-flame.

The best way to seek spiritual healing is to offer gratitude every day for a fleeting second to the Supreme Healer. When we offer our gratitude to Him for what we have or for what we are right now, then our heart of aspiration and dedication expands. That means that our receptivity increases. When receptivity increases, God's Light, which is all healing, can enter into us in abundant measure. It is in the heart of gratitude that God's Light can permanently abide.

If your gratitude-sun
Meditates on God,
Then God will give Himself to you
Entirely.

Illness is all around. How can we cure it? We can cure it only through our gratitude-heart.

We have to offer our gratitude to the Absolute Supreme that He has given us the sincere inner cry to cure humanity's suffering. There are many who do not care to cure illness either within themselves or within the world. There are many millions and billions of people on earth, but how many are crying to cure the sufferings and ills of mankind? Very few. Just because we are seekers, we are crying and trying to cure the age-old illnesses and sufferings of mankind. Who has given us this aspiration, this inner cry? God Himself. So it is our bounden duty to offer Him our gratitude. Who has given us this capacity? God Himself. At every moment, if we can offer our gratitude to God, then the receptivity of our heart increases. And inside our receptivity is strength, light and power to cure the sufferings of mankind.

Something new happened
This morning:
I meditated on the Supreme
Unconditionally.
Something new shall happen
This evening:
My life shall grow into
A gratitude-heart.

Cry within powerfully. Smile without soulfully.

We bring gratitude to the fore through our constant inner cry. We cry outwardly when we desperately need name, fame, outer capacity, prosperity and so forth. But when we cry inwardly, we have to feel that we are crying only to please and fulfil God in His own way. The outer cry is for our own fulfilment, in our own way. The inner cry is for God-fulfilment in God's own way. If there is a constant inner cry, that means we are trying to please God, satisfy God and fulfil God in God's own way. If we can cry inwardly, in silence, then our gratitude increases because inside the inner cry is the abode of gratitude, and inside the abode of gratitude is God.

Smaller than the smallest
May be the outer temple
Where every day I go to worship my Lord.
But larger than the largest
Is my inner temple
Where every day I go to pray and meditate
With my aspiration-cry and dedication-smile
To become another God.

Are you tired of being who you are? Then give God, for the first time, a chance to take care of you. God can easily take care of you and He will definitely do it. Just give Him a chance.

To realise that only God's Will can give you happiness, just see what happens when you fulfil your own will. It is all frustration. When you fulfil God's Will, you get only joy. After you have experienced this a few times, you have enough proof. When you have fulfilled your own desires or achieved something in your own way, have you really got satisfaction? Immediately the answer will be no. But God's way will definitely give you satisfaction.

Remembrance is painful
When I see that in vain
My sweet Lord tried to change me.
Remembrance is delightful
When at long last
I have surrendered my orphan-will
To God's omnipotent Will.

Soulful happiness is my escort. Therefore, I shall go very far.

If you are happy, it will help your spiritual progress to a great extent. If you are unhappy, you will not make any progress at all. On the contrary, you will be marching backwards. Real outer happiness is not self-deception. It does not come from wasting time and indulging in pleasure-life. Real outer happiness is something totally different. It comes from inner joy and inner satisfaction.

If you want to make progress,
Only think of your heart's happiness
And how you can keep
Your entire being happy.
Wherever you go,
Carry happiness with you.

Man's sincere desire: grasp, possess and enjoy quickly. The soul's sincere desire: aspire, offer and enjoy eternally.

In this world either we desire or we aspire. At each moment we are given ample opportunity to possess and grab the world or to become inseparably one with the world. Meditation teaches us how to become inseparably one with the world at large. When we cry for the Vast, for the ultimate Truth, meditation is the immediate answer. When we want to achieve boundless peace, boundless light, boundless bliss, meditation is the only answer. The world needs one thing—peace—and meditation is the only answer.

A soulful moment of powerful meditation
Is an answer
To a day of ruthless confusion-thoughts.

**Prayer is the secret of tremendous success.
Meditation is the secret of precious progress.**

Meditation and prayer are two different types of conversation, but they serve the same purpose. When we pray, we talk to God; we tell Him all about our needs and all our soulful expectations. Through our prayer we ask God for anything that we want, and anything that we would like to offer God from our very existence we offer through our prayer. But when we meditate, we remain silent, absolutely silent, and we beg of God to work in and through us. He dictates and we try to execute His express Will.

Lord Supreme,
You have helped me
To speak to You.
Let me help You
By listening to You.

Each prayer is divinely important. Each meditation is supremely significant. Each experience is soulfully fruitful.

In the beginning, we see and feel on the strength of our meditation that God alone is doing everything and that we are mere instruments. But in time, when we go deep within, we come to realise that He is not only the Doer but also the action itself, and He is not only the action but also the result thereof. To simplify the matter, we can say that meditation means God's conscious and compassionate dictates to us, and prayer means our soulful conversation with God. When we meditate, God talks to us and we most devotedly listen. When we pray, we talk to God and He most compassionately listens.

When I meditate on God,
I see Him on
The wings of silence.
When I pray to God,
I see Him inside
The cave of sound.

Your mind has a flood of questions. There is but one teacher who can answer them. Who is the teacher? Your silence-loving heart.

There are two significant roads that can lead us toward our destined Goal. One road is the mental road, the road of the mind; the other is the psychic road, the road of the heart. Both of these roads will take us to our destined Goal, but one road is shorter and safer, and that is the road of the heart. When we follow the road of the mind, at any moment doubt can snatch us away. The world's information can pull down our aspiration. But the road of the heart is sunlit. When we follow this road, we always feel deep within us a deer running towards the destined Goal.

My heart is gazing into
Tomorrow's distance-light.
It is empty of even
A speck of fear.

In his restless hours, he meditates on God unconditionally. In his peaceful hours, he meditates on himself, the future God.

If one is sincere and really aspiring, he prays and meditates in a divine way, according to his capacity. He does what he can, and at the same time he watches all the situations, calamities and forces around him. He says, "I have done my part. Now it is up to God to free me from these undivine forces or unpleasant experiences." This is the best attitude. If we can go deep within every day during our meditation, we will become the observer, the witness. But if we cannot go deep within every day in our meditation, the next best thing is to act like a hero and offer the results of our actions to God. The result may take the form of defeat. But if we can gladly offer the result to God, we are acting like a divine hero.

No difference, none,
Between a divine hero
And a supreme doer.

No difference, none,
Between a supreme doer
And a God-satisfaction-lover.

If you become an absolutely sincere seeker, then no matter where you are or with whom you are, you are bound to feel an inner cry. This inner cry can and will become constant if your heart is nothing but sincerity and purity.

When you work every day with people who are not aspiring, you can maintain your high aspiration in the same way that the best student in the class manages to study with bad students. The best student knows that he has a goal. He has to learn his lesson thoroughly, he has to please his teacher, he has to be inundated with knowledge-light; whereas the bad students are either totally ignorant of these things or they do not care for these things. Similarly, while you are working with unaspiring people, you have to give all your attention to your inner life of aspiration. You have to feel that your life of aspiration has a definite goal: realisation of the highest Absolute.

Your aspiration-life
Will definitely be blessed
With God-intoxication.
It is only a matter
Of fleeting time!

God wants to be the first person to applaud your inner illumination and outer transformation.

One way to transform human nature is to bring down the divine, all-illumining light of the Supreme, enlarging one's receptivity-vessel. Before human nature is transformed, it is full of darkness. Darkness can be removed only by bringing in light and not by anything else. We have to bring down light from above consciously and constantly and then expand our receptivity. The more we expand our receptivity, the more we can hold light inside ourselves.

Slowly the mind
Becomes clean.
Steadily the heart
Becomes pure.
Unconditionally the soul
Manifests the Supreme.
Supremely our Beloved Supreme
Fulfils Himself
In and through His creation-child.

It is never too late to transform one's nature completely.

Another way to transform human nature is to see the divine light in each human being and nothing else. Just because we see something undivine in ourselves and in others, it has become impossible for us to transform either our own nature or human nature in general. No matter what they do, what they say or what they are, if we consciously and constantly see only the divine light in others—the light we are bringing down from above—then automatically human nature will be transformed. If we see light in each individual and in our own nature, then it is not only possible but also inevitable to transform human nature and earth's nature.

Face your lower nature
Bravely.
Your higher nature
Is about to reach you
Happily
Plus proudly.

True humility means giving joy to others.

If you have not established or cannot establish your inner oneness with others, then you can try to make them feel that they are as important as you, if not more so. On the outer plane if you can make people feel that they are really important, then they will value you. Here on earth we want to get joy. But how do we get joy? We get joy not by coming forward before others, but by bringing others to the fore. Real joy we get by self-giving, not by possessing or by showing our own supremacy. When we allow others to get joy first, then we feel that our joy is more complete, more perfect, more divine. By making others feel that they are either equally important or more important, we show our true humility.

If your life does not give joy
To others,
Then how can you expect
Your heart to give any joy
To you?

We have to breathe in purity as we breathe in air. We have to think of purity consciously.

We have an inner existence and we have an outer existence. Our inner existence is bound to be suffocated when it is impossible for us to breathe in purity. The cosmic Self, the universal Self, is always eager to supply us with purity in infinite measure. If purity is not established in our inner life, our outer life is bound to fail sooner or later. In purity our divinity can grow; in purity our true life can flourish and have its fulfilment here on earth.

It is purity
And not insecurity
That has to take full possession
Of your heart.

Because of your merciless ambition, you will forever remain an unfinished creation.

Where there is ambition, there is always an unfortunate competitive spirit. You are ambitious because you want to surpass someone; you want to achieve something which others have not achieved. When there is ambition, there is a great danger that you will not go toward your real goal. Ambition may take you to a destination which is not your real destination but somebody else's destination. Because the song of ambition is the song of superiority over others, consciously or unconsciously it takes us to another goal. But when you are aspiring, you are not aspiring just because others are aspiring or because you want to outdo them in aspiration. No! Here there is no competitive spirit. It is your own inner absolute necessity that you are fulfilling. You are aspiring because you feel that it is your bounden duty to reach your destined goal, so that you can be of greatest service to the Absolute Supreme.

You have lost
Your beloved Satisfaction-God
Because you have overfed
Your insistent ambition-horse.

Competition is good, provided it is the competition of self-transcendence and not the competition of ego-demonstration.

When there is aspiration there is oneness, and in oneness there is no need of competition. But if there is no aspiration and no sense of oneness, if someone is in the desire-world, then naturally ambition has to play its role. Before we enter into the spiritual life, ambition is a help, but that ambition eventually becomes a great obstacle, a real enemy, if it is not transformed into pure aspiration once we accept the spiritual life.

An aspiration-heart
Does not need an outer record,
For its very existence on earth
Is its supreme record.

Nobody can see God on his own terms.

We cannot define God in terms of one specific feeling or experience. Each one has to experience God for himself. If we say God is all peace or God is all delight, then there will be people to contradict us. Each one has to define God for himself. We all want to have satisfaction. I have satisfaction by experiencing truth and light, and others will also derive satisfaction from that reality-experience, although they may call it by a different name.

Do not try to make God
Into your image.
He will please you,
But your ignorance-choice
Will make you suffer
Far beyond your imagination's flight
During your darkness-enjoying journey.

All eyes will be on you when your own eyes look within and drink deep the delight of your universal oneness-heart.

We are all God's children. We speak in different languages, but when it is a matter of the heart—your heart, my heart, his heart, her heart—we are all in tune. It is only the mind that creates problems. The aspiring heart is constantly in communication with the soul, and the soul is the representative of God. There is always an abiding truth inside all of us. When it is a matter of real spirituality, there is no geographical barrier—no east, no west, no north, no south. There is only the heart's oneness. It is through our heart's oneness that we fulfil ourselves and fulfil God in and through us.

When you are right,
Everything around you is right,
Because the beautiful flow
That is inside your heart
Has the capacity to spread
Its fragrance of oneness-light
Around you.

A self-giving heart will, without fail, win what it so rightly deserves.

We are all instruments of God. But if we are too much involved in the material life, then we will not be able to be chosen instruments of God. Chosen instruments of God are those who are constantly self-giving. They are not for themselves but for the entire world. Chosen instruments have a wide heart. They do not try to confine themselves to their own reality. They try to offer their lives to the world at large.

There is only one highway to Heaven,
And that highway
Is our constant and unconditional
Self-giving way.

DECEMBER

How to invite your own spiritual death?
Make friends with
Self-satisfied complacency.
How to prove you are a real God-seeker?
Climb higher and dive deeper
To transcend your teeming weaknesses.

Do you want to succeed enormously? Then adjust your outer mind. Do you want to proceed confidently? Then harmonise your inner life.

In order to acquire harmony, one needs peace of mind. In order to have peace of mind, one needs to meditate most soulfully on the Inner Pilot, who has created the necessity for inner harmony. If one meditates properly, then peace of mind and harmony will be reflected in all one's outer movements. When the mind has peace, then there is always harmony in all the activities which take place in one's being.

My heart and my mind
Have renewed their friendship.
My heart of love
Shall show my mind the way.
My mind of peace
Shall guard my heart
Along the way.

Hope is nothing but concealed power. Today's hope turns into tomorrow's actuality. Today's dream is bound to be fulfilled in tomorrow's reality.

As hope is a power, so also expectation is a power. We expect many things from ourselves and from the world. We feel that today's expectation is going to bring down tomorrow's realisation. But in the spiritual life, we play our role without any expectation whatsoever. We feel that our role is to perform divine service, but not to expect the fruits thereof. If we can love, serve, pray and meditate with utmost sincerity, purity and self-offering, then our God-appointed realisation is bound to dawn. This realisation will far transcend our highest expectation and far surpass the flights of our loftiest imagination.

Self-imprisonment begins
The day we start playing
With expectation-snare
And never, never before.

Human nature does not change and cannot change without selfless service.

Selfless service contains the supreme secret of oneness with God's Will. Before we do something, we have to feel that a divine force is acting in and through us. Then when we do the thing and get the result either in the form of failure or success, we have to feel that this is the experience that the Supreme wants us to have and we have to become one with that experience. If it is failure, we take it as an experience. If it is success, we also take it as an experience. Always we have to be one with the result and offer it at the Feet of the Supreme. In this way we make the fastest progress.

Do not wait!
If you really want God
To be always on your side,
Then immediately choose to serve.

To lessen world tension, each seeker-heart must feed the peace-starving humanity.

In this world there is a need for peace. This peace comes only from within, and we can bring it to the fore only through meditation. If we can meditate soulfully for ten minutes every day, we will energise our entire being with peace. Peace houses light, bliss, fulfilment and satisfaction. We can have peace not by possessing the world or leading the world, but by becoming a lover of the world.

My Lord,
My love of the world is unconditional.
But how far can it take me?
"My child,
It can easily take you all the way."

If you are caught by the expectation-chain, how can you escape the powerful blows of despair-night?

At the beginning, we demand everything from the world in return for our offering, our life of sacrifice. If we give something, we expect the same amount in return, if not more. Then there comes a time when we give as much as we have, we give to the utmost of our capacity, and we expect in return only an infinitesimal measure of what we have given. But even if we expect just an infinitesimal quantity of appreciation from the world, I wish to say that we are bound to be unhappy; we are bound to be wanting in peace. Let us give to the world unconditionally what we have and what we are: love. The message of love we get only from our daily prayer and meditation. We know that love means oneness, inseparable oneness. And in oneness there is no expectation, no demand.

If your mind still has
Chains of expectation,
You will definitely be doomed
To dire disappointments.

Peace is not to be found in external knowledge. Most of our external knowledge is founded on information, and information cannot give us any abiding satisfaction. Peace is not to be found in outer efficiency. Peace is found in self-mastery.

Peace is our inner wealth. This inner wealth we can bring to the fore only when we expect nothing from the outer world and everything from the Supreme Pilot within us at His choice Hour. Often when we serve the world, we feel that it is the world's bounden duty to offer us gratitude or to acknowledge our service. When we expect something from the world, we are bound to meet with frustration. But when we expect from the Inner Pilot, He fulfils us beyond the flight of our imagination.

Deep within us
Is the seed of perfect perfection.
We must wait for God's choice Hour.
At that time the perfection-seed
Will definitely germinate.

Today's proud ambition tomorrow becomes a helpless victim to itself.

When ambition becomes our bosom friend, when our inner being is surcharged with determination, we achieve success. But we have to realise that when we surrender our ambition to the Source, we make true progress, and in this progress we find real fulfilment. When we succeed in something in the outer world, we feel that we have done it in spite of opposition from the entire world. We feel that it is by virtue of our own capacities that we have achieved our desired success. But when we make progress—no matter in which field—within the inmost recesses of our heart we come to feel that the entire world helped us, that each individual on earth has helped us in some way or other according to his capacity.

In the vital world
Every day I used my ambition-mind
To make my life happy.
Now in the psychic world
All the time I use
My aspiration-heart
To make myself happy.

Failure indicates our lack of adamantine determination. Success indicates our tremendous power of concentration. Progress indicates that the crown of God's Will is in us and for us.

In our day-to-day life when we fail in something, we feel that our whole world is lost. We find it extremely hard to bury our sad experience in oblivion. When we succeed, at times we are bloated with pride. We cherish this pride because of our ego. At times we exaggerate our achievement beyond imagination. At times we want to prove to the world that we have or we are something when, in the purest sense of the term, it is not true. We try to make others feel we are exceptional, but in the inmost recesses of our heart we know that this is false. When we care for progress, we want to be only what God wants us to be. We do not want any appreciation whatsoever from the world. We do not want the world to overestimate or underestimate us; we just want the world to accept us.

Who can determine
The distance between
My known years of failure
And my unknown years of success,
If not the truth-seeker in me
And the God-lover in me?

Do not worry! He who worries buries himself with the unsolicited help of today's powerful hands and tomorrow's indifferent eyes.

Let us not worry over the future. Let us think of the present. As you sow, so you reap. In the past perhaps you have not sown the proper seed. Let us say your inner cry was not intense in the past and that is why your aspiration is not strong now. If you sow a seed now, it will germinate and become a plant and eventually grow into a giant banyan tree. So if we sow the proper seed—that is to say, aspiration—then the aspiration-tree will bear fruit, which we call realisation. But if we do not sow the proper seed inside ourselves, then how can we get the proper fruit? So let us not worry about the future. Let us only do the right thing today, at this moment, here and now. Try to aspire now, today, and let the future take care of itself.

Because I am a truth-seeker,
The future flows towards me.
Because I am a God-lover,
I live in the eternal Now.

Do not allow tension to stab your life if you want to succeed in your prayer-life and proceed in your manifestation-life.

We can have more joy and less tension in our daily life only by self-giving, not by demanding. When there is tension, it is because we want something to be done in our own way while others want it done in their way. Tension starts in the mind because we see light in one way and others see light in some other way. So there is no peace, no poise, only tension. Tension also comes when we want to do something in the twinkling of an eye that takes two hours or two days to do. We have to know that God has not thought of it in that way. God wants us to take two hours or two days to achieve it. If we can keep God's Hour in our minds and not our own hour, we will get joy. Tension goes away from the seeker's mind when he knows the art of surrendering to God's Will.

Let your heart
Tell your mind
That God is in full control
Of your life.
You will immediately see
That your tension has ceased
And your confidence
Has powerfully returned.

What is joy? It is a bird that we all want to catch. It is the same bird that we all love to see flying.

We must see that God operates not only in us but in others as well. God also operates in our so-called enemies. But these are not our real enemies. Our real enemies are our doubt, fear, anxiety and worry. When we do not cry to perfect others, but only try to perfect our own lives, then we will have joy. Also, if we do not expect anything from anybody else but expect everything only from God, then we will get joy. If we can feel that we are not indispensable, that without us the world can go on perfectly well, then we will have joy. This is the way we can all get abundant joy in our spiritual life.

You will find no joy in your mind-cave,
No matter how many times a day
You enter it.
Joy is where your loving heart is.
Joy is where your strong life is.

Conscious self-examination is the most auspicious beginning of God-realisation.

God-realisation means self-discovery in the highest sense of the term. One consciously realises his oneness with God. As long as the seeker remains in ignorance, he will feel that God is somebody else who has infinite power, while he, the seeker, is the feeblest person on earth. But the moment he realises God, he comes to know that he and God are absolutely one in both the inner and the outer life. God-realisation means one's identification with one's absolute highest Self. When one can identify with one's highest Self and remain in that consciousness forever, when one can reveal and manifest it at one's own command, that is God-realisation.

There are two kinds of responsibility.
One is preparation
And the other is realisation.
Preparation is your responsibility.
Realisation is God's responsibility.

Is hell on this earth? The doubting mind has and is the only answer. Is Heaven on this earth? The aspiring heart has and is the only answer.

Heaven and God are not high above us, somewhere far away; they are deep within us, inside our hearts. Heaven is not a distant country where there are trees and houses and other objects; it is a plane of consciousness within us. Seekers of the eternal Truth will realise their eternal Heaven within their aspiring hearts. At every moment we are creating Heaven or hell within us. When we cherish a divine thought, an expanding thought, a fulfilling thought, we create Heaven in us. When we cherish undivine, ugly, obscure, impure thoughts, we enter into our own inner hell.

Question your mind dauntlessly.
Search your heart carefully.
You will be able to fathom Heaven
Inside your dedication-life.

In your early morning meditation, be regular, be punctual and be sincere.

Meditation needs practice. You have to practise to become spontaneous in your meditation. Why is it that you get hungry one day and the next day you do not get hungry? If you work hard on the outer plane, then you are bound to become hungry. If, on the physical plane, you run quite a few miles, then you are bound to feel hungry. Similarly, if you work hard on the inner plane, then you will be blessed with receptivity. On the inner plane, if you cry soulfully and devotedly, then you can create receptivity, and inside that receptivity you will feel gratitude. When you feel gratitude, at that time your meditation is bound to be spontaneous.

It is infinitely more difficult
For a sincere truth-seeker
And a true God-lover
To remain asleep
Than to wake up early in the morning
At God's choice Hour
To meditate.

All roads lead to something. That something can be either your life's destruction-cry or your heart's perfection-smile.

With our human ego we try to establish oneness with others. We feel that we have more capacity than others, so therefore we are entitled to oneness with them. But if we try to use ego as an instrument to establish oneness, then we will never succeed. Our oneness with others entirely depends on our soulful love. If we use the reasoning mind, then we can never discover love within us. If we use the demanding vital, then we can never discover love within us. But if we use the loving, fulfilling heart, then oneness becomes a reality in our day-to-day life.

Every day collect love-flowers
From your heart-garden
And place them on your soul's
Peace-shrine
As a prayer to your Beloved Supreme.

Only one quality can solve all your problems and that quality is called gratitude-heart.

Every day count the petals of your gratitude-heart and every day offer another petal to the Supreme. If you want to name the individual petals, you can call them simplicity, purity, humility and so forth. But think of the heart itself as gratitude. That is the only quality that will help all seekers not only to solve their problems, but also to run the fastest in the spiritual life.

Nothing else is perfect
And
Nothing else can ever be perfect
Except the soulful cry
Of our fruitful gratitude-heart.

In the spiritual life there should be no fear.

If you are praying to God the Almighty, meditating on God the Almighty, why should you be afraid of anything or anyone? A child feels his mother has all the power of the world. When he is afraid of anything he runs to his mother because the mother has all affection for him. Here also, you are a spiritual child of God, so when you are attacked by any kind of fear—either on the physical, the mental or the vital plane—immediately try to run towards your sweet Supreme, who is all Compassion, all Love, all Blessings.

If you really want to please God
In God's own way,
Then you must never have
A whisper of fear
Inside the breath of your faith.

There are only two misfortunes in life: one is that we do not know what to do, and the other is that we cannot forget what we have done.

We do something wrong out of ignorance and then we have a guilty conscience because of our wrongdoing. Instead, the first thing that should come to our mind is, "If I have the power to do something wrong, then God has the power to forgive me." When we have done something very bad we must not feel that there is no power in the universe to obliterate our wrong deeds. We have done something wrong, granted, but God is infinitely stronger than we are, and we should remember that He is all Compassion. Whenever we meditate we should feel that God is all Love. He is not going to punish us. With His infinite Compassion He is going to transform us. But if we cherish a feeling of guilt, God will not be able to come to our rescue.

You want your guilty mind to hide,
But God wants to bring
Your guilty mind to light
So that someday He can enjoy
Its transformation-perfection-height.

~December 19 ~

Purity is the seeker's inner sunshine to cure his outer life of division-malady.

If we are really pure, then we do not see impurity in others. If we are not pure, then we see mud in everybody. Real spiritual people are not at all disturbed by impurity, because they have tremendous inner light and that light saves them. So, do not seek impurity in others; only think of your own inner light. The more you can bring to the fore your inner light, either the impurity you see will be illumined or you will not see impurity at all.

A man of purity
Does not have to know
How to approach the world,
For his Lord Supreme
Approaches the world
In and through him.

If you want to love God and therefore want to serve God, then your soulful service is more precious to God than you can ever imagine.

Dedicated, devoted service is of paramount importance. This service can be of various types: it can be physical work or it can take the form of an offering of devoted thoughts, ideas, love and concern. Physically you can do dedicated service and spiritually you can do dedicated service. Financially and materially also you can do dedicated service. Each person can be the Supreme's true divine pride. Physical service, vital service, mental service, psychic service and soul's service can be offered at the Feet of the Supreme. The greatest service is to have conscious, surrendered oneness with the Supreme. But all these other types of service do help considerably in entering the unconditionally surrendered life. Start where you are now and each moment offer your dedicated service to the Supreme.

My Lord Supreme,
My heart has a special prayer:
I long to be
Consciously and constantly useful
In Your service-light
And for Your Eye's
Sole satisfaction-delight.

In the spiritual life, nothing is as important as enthusiasm. When one loses one's enthusiasm, one loses everything.

When we launch into the spiritual life, we need enthusiasm. Without it we will not budge an inch. Enthusiasm is very good, but over-eagerness is bad. If we eat beyond our capacity, we will suffer from indigestion. We must not feel that we will be able to realise God overnight, or that we are running a competition where we are trying to beat everybody. We are competing only with our own ignorance. We need patience as well as enthusiasm to win the race.

Relax,
Relax soulfully,
Relax powerfully.
You are bound to feel
An inflow of creative energy
And constructive enthusiasm.

Changes in our aspiration-life have to be accepted as soulfully and cheerfully as the inspiring and absorbing changes in the seasons.

When aspiration is wavering, we find it difficult to go deep within. We hate to meditate and even if we meditate, our meditation is not good. What should we do at that time? We should read inspiring books written by God-realised souls or other seekers who are searching for God. Then we should feel the seeker we are reading about is no one else but ourself. We should feel each idea, each thought or heart's cry of aspiration as our own. The writer has used his name, but it is our feeling that he has written about, our own aspiration. When we read the seeker's devoted writings, we should feel that his cry is our cry. As he is going towards light, we should feel that we also want to go towards light.

My heart gets aspiration
Only when I choose
The right thing to become.
What is the right thing to become?
I shall become God's
Most perfect instrument.

Spirituality is not like coasting, but exactly like climbing—climbing ten thousand Himalayas.

We have to know that the spiritual life is neither a bed of thorns nor a bed of roses. There are always deserts in life's journey. Everybody has to go through the desert in his aspiration, but there comes a time when there is no desert. Daylight is followed by night and again night by day. But a time comes in our inner aspiration when we enter into a deeper consciousness, a deeper being, and we become one with our soul. When we are able to listen to the dictates of our soul, when we are in communion with God, then our consciousness is full of light. Each thought, each idea is full of light. Then there is no night. It is all light. That is the very highest state.

The spiritual life is arduous.
But the sincere seekers
Who will ultimately hold
The banners of divine light
And supreme delight
Will forever and forever remain faithful
To their inner Captain.

The aim of life is to become conscious of the Supreme Reality. The aim of life is to be the conscious expression of the Eternal Being.

There are two lives: the inner life and the outer life. The outer life speaks about its principles and then tries to act. It professes in season and out of season, but it practises very little of what it professes. The inner life does not speak. It acts. Its spontaneous action is the conscious manifestation of God.

If you have an inner will,
Then use it properly.
Use it to control
Your outer life.
If you have an outer will,
Then use it properly.
Use it to feed and please
Your inner life.

It requires a giant exercise of faith to manifest the oneness-bond of man with God.

We have to jump courageously into the ocean of spirituality, but we have to know that we are not jumping into the sea of uncertainty. Uncertainty and spirituality never go together. When we speak of courage, we have to know that courage means certainty. It is not by hook or by crook that we are going to realise God. It is through our constant self-offering. Self-offering is the most powerful weapon, for it is in self-offering that true courage lies. When we know that God is ours and we are God's, we feel spontaneous courage streaming forth.

Self-offering
Is the only supreme secret
That can help you with
A thick book of God-victories.

Keep your mind centred on God. Your futile thoughts will be transformed into fertile ideas, your fertile ideas into glowing ideals and your glowing ideals into all-fulfilling Infinitude.

We have to be a divine potter with the dirty clay of our thoughts. If the potter is afraid to touch the clay, if he refuses to touch it, then the clay will remain clay and the potter will not be able to offer anything to the world. But the potter is not afraid. He touches the clay and shapes it into something beautiful and useful. Like this, it is our bounden duty to transform undivine thoughts.

Each base thought
Defiles everything that is sacred
Immediately.
Each pure thought
Immortalises everything that is willing to change
Unmistakably and unreservedly.

There is no other way to please our inner self than to be a perfect emblem of courage.

Courage is absolutely necessary in the spiritual life. The very acceptance of the spiritual life demands enormous courage. It is only a divinely courageous soul, only a divinely inspired soul, that can swiftly reach the highest Goal. This courage is not the courage of a haughty, rough person who will strike others to assert his superiority. This courage is our constant awareness of what we are entering into, of what we are going to become, of what we are going to reveal.

A divinely ambitious life,
A supremely courageous heart
And
An unconditionally gracious God
Enjoy a permanent friendship.

Surrender, surrender, constantly surrender to God's Will. You will then have zooming self-confidence.

Doubt will leave us only when we feel that we are destined to do something for God. We get tremendous power from the word "destined." This word brings boundless courage to the fore. Even if somebody is weak by nature, if someone says that he is destined to work for God, then immediately, from the inner world, heroism comes forward. He will fight against any obstruction with a strength and inner determination that will surprise him. Obstructions may come to him in the form of impurity, obscurity, jealousy, fear and doubt, but the word "destined" will smash the pride of all the negative forces. Anything that is undivine will have to surrender to this word. So if we have the inner and outer conviction that we are destined to serve God, then the Goal can unmistakably be reached.

I was born to do something
Really great for God
On this planet.
How can I fail?
Why should I fail?

Life has an inner lamp. This inner lamp is called aspiration. When we keep our aspiration burning, it will, without fail, transmit to God's entire creation its effulgent glow.

Aspiration is the inner flame. Unlike other flames, this flame does not burn anything. It purifies, illumines and transforms our life. When purification takes place in our lower nature, we hope to see the Face of God. When illumination dawns in our outer nature, we feel that God is near and dear, that He is all-pervading and all-loving. When our nature, both lower and outer, grows into a transformation-flame, we shall realise the truth that God Himself is the inmost Pilot, brightest Journey and highest Goal.

A completely new vision:
My aspiration-flame,
No matter how weak and feeble,
Can never be doomed to a failure-life.
A life of success
Lovingly, cheerfully and proudly
Awaits my aspiration-life.

In the life of aspiration, between fear and doubt, choose neither; between faith and surrender, choose both.

At every moment you have to aim at your goal. If you want to concentrate and meditate on the sun as it rises early in the morning, then you have to face the east, and not some other direction. If you are looking toward the west and running toward the east, you will stumble. If you want to be certain of your goal of God-realisation, then you will not look behind you or around you, but only toward the light. You can conquer your desires only by running toward the light. do not think of your desires, but think only of your aspiration. If you can run forward with one-pointed determination, limitations and desires will fade away from your life. Aspiration is the only answer. For outer things you cry; for inner things you can also cry. If you can cry sincerely, you can fly spiritually.

When I think, I sink.
When I choose, I lose.
When I cry, I fly.

In the world of aspiration there are many roads, but all roads lead to the same goal: God, the Absolute Supreme.

With aspiration we begin our journey, and with aspiration we continue our journey. Since there is no end to our journey, and since God is infinite, eternal and immortal, our aspiration will constantly flow toward God's Infinity, Eternity and Immortality. Aspiration is the endless road that eternally leads toward the ever-transcending Beyond.

A desire-life
Is my strange life.
An aspiration-life
Is my hard-earned life.
A realisation-life
Shall be my absolutely normal life.

INDEX

417

About the Author

S RI CHINMOY IS A FULLY REALISED SPIRITUAL Master dedicated to serving those seeking a deeper meaning in life. Through his teaching of meditation, his music, art and writings, his athletics and his own life of dedicated service to humanity, he tries to inspire others in their search for inner peace and fulfilment.

Born in Bengal in 1931, Sri Chinmoy entered an ashram (spiritual community) at the age of 12. His life of intense spiritual practice included meditating for up to 14 hours a day, together with writing poetry, essays and devotional songs, doing selfless service and practising athletics. While still in his early teens, he had many profound inner experiences and attained spiritual realisation. He remained in the ashram for 20 years, deepening and expanding his realisation, and in 1964 came to New York City to share his inner wealth with sincere seekers.

Today, Sri Chinmoy serves as a spiritual guide to disciples in some 250 centres around the world. He advocates the "Path of the Heart" as the simplest way to make rapid spiritual progress. By meditating on the spiritual heart, he teaches, the seeker can discover his own inner treasures of peace, joy, light and love. The role of a spiritual Master, according to Sri Chinmoy, is to help the seeker live so that these inner riches can illumine his life. He instructs his disciples in the inner life and elevates their consciousness not only beyond their expectation, but even beyond their imagination. In return he asks his students to meditate regularly and to try to nurture their inner qualities.

Sri Chinmoy teaches that love is the most direct way for a seeker to approach the Supreme. When a child feels love for his father, it does not matter how great the father is in the world's eye; through his love the child feels only his oneness with his father and his father's possessions. This same approach, applied to the Supreme, permits the seeker to feel that the Supreme and His own Eternity, Infinity and Immortality are the seeker's own. This philosophy of love, Sri Chinmoy feels, expresses the deepest bond between man and God, who are aspects of the same unified consciousness. In the life-game, man fulfils himself in the Supreme by realising that the Supreme is man's own highest self. The Supreme reveals Himself through man, who serves as His instrument for world transformation and perfection.

In the traditional Indian fashion, Sri Chinmoy does not charge a fee for his spiritual guidance, nor does he charge for his frequent concerts or public meditations. His only fee, he says, is the seeker's sincere inner cry. He takes a personal interest in each of his students, and when he accepts a disciple, he takes full responsibility for that seeker's inner progress. In New York, Sri Chinmoy meditates in person with his disciples several times a week and offers a regular weekly meditation session for the general public. Students living outside New York see Sri Chinmoy during worldwide gatherings that take place three times a year, during visits to New York, or during the Master's trips to their cities. They find that the inner bond between Master and disciple transcends physical separation. Sri Chinmoy accepts students at all levels of development, from beginners to advanced seekers, and lovingly guides them inwardly and outwardly according to their individual needs.

Sri Chinmoy's life demonstrates most vividly that spirituality is not an escape from the world, but a means of transforming it. He has written more than 1000 books, which include plays, poems, stories, essays, commentaries and answers to questions on spirituality. He has painted thousands of widely exhibited mystical paintings and composed more than 13,000 devotional songs. Performing his own compositions on a wide variety of instruments, he has offered a series of several hundred Peace Concerts in cities around the world.

A naturally gifted athlete and a firm believer in the spiritual benefits of physical fitness, Sri Chinmoy encourages his disciples to participate in sports. Under his inspirational guidance, the international Sri Chinmoy Marathon Team organises hundreds of road races, including the longest certified running race in the world (1,300 miles), and stages a global relay run for peace every two years.

Sri Chinmoy's achievements as a weightlifter have also earned him considerable renown. To demonstrate that inner peace gained through meditation can be a tangible source of outer strength, he has lifted objects weighing as much as 7,000 pounds using only one arm. In addition, he has honoured more than 2,000 individuals by physically lifting them overhead on a specially constructed platform in an awards programme entitled "Lifting Up the World with a Oneness-Heart."

For further information, please write to:
AUM PUBLICATIONS
86-10 Parsons Blvd. • Jamaica, N.Y. 11432

ADDITIONAL TITLES
by Sri Chinmoy

Meditation: Man-Perfection in God-Satisfaction

Presented with the simplicity and clarity that have become the hallmark of Sri Chinmoy's writings, this book is easily one of the most comprehensive guides to meditation available.

Topics include: Proven meditation techniques that anyone can learn • How to still the restless mind • Developing the power of concentration • Carrying peace with you always • Awakening the heart centre to discover the power of your soul • The significance of prayer. Plus a special section in which Sri Chinmoy answers questions on a wide range of experiences often encountered in meditation. $9.95

Beyond Within: A Philosophy for the Inner Life

"How can I carry on the responsibilities of life and still grow inwardly to find spiritual fulfilment?"

When your simple yearning to know the purpose of your life and feel the reality of God has you swimming against the tide, then the wisdom and guidance of a spiritual Master who has crossed these waters is priceless. Sri Chinmoy offers profound insight into man's relationship with God, and sound advice on how to integrate the highest spiritual aspirations into daily life.

Topics include: The transformation and perfection of the body • The spiritual journey • Meditation • The relationship between the mind and physical illness • Using the soul's will to conquer life's problems • How you can throw away guilt • Overcoming fear of failure • The purpose of pain and suffering • Becoming conscious of your own divine nature • The occult. $13.95

Death and Reincarnation

This deeply moving book has brought consolation and understanding to countless people faced with the loss of a loved one or fear of their own mortality. Sri Chinmoy explains the secrets of death, the afterlife and reincarnation. $7.95

Kundalini: The Mother-Power

En route to his own spiritual realisation, Sri Chinmoy attained mastery over the Kundalini and occult powers. In this book he explains techniques for awakening the Kundalini and the chakras. He warns of the dangers and pitfalls to be avoided and discusses some of the occult powers that come with the opening of the chakras. $7.95

Yoga and the Spiritual Life

Specifically tailored for Western readers, this book offers rare insight into the philosophy of Yoga and Eastern mysticism. It offers novices as well as advanced seekers a deep understanding of the spiritual side of life. Of particular interest is the section on the soul and the inner life. $8.95

The Summits of God-Life: Samadhi and Siddhi
A genuine account of the world beyond time and space

This is Sri Chinmoy's firsthand account of states of consciousness that only a handful of Masters have ever experienced. Not a theoretical or philosophical book, but a vivid and detailed description of the farthest possibilities of human consciousness. Essential reading for all seekers longing to fulfil their own spiritual potential. $6.95

Inner and Outer Peace

A powerful yet simple approach for establishing peace in your own life and the world.

Sri Chinmoy speaks of the higher truths that energise the quest for world peace, giving contemporary expression to the relationship between our personal search for inner peace and the world's search for outer peace. He reveals truths which lift the peace of the world above purely political and historical considerations, contributing his spiritual understanding and inspiration to the cause of world peace. $7.95

Eastern Light for the Western Mind
Sri Chinmoy's University Talks

In the summer of 1970, in the midst of the social and political upheavals that were sweeping college campuses, Sri Chinmoy embarked on a university lecture tour offering the message of peace and hope embodied in Eastern philosophy. Speaking in a state of deep meditation, he filled the audience with a peace and serenity many had

never before experienced. They found his words, as a faculty member later put it, "to be living seeds of spirituality." These moments are faithfully captured in this beautiful volume of 42 talks.
$7.95

A Child's Heart and a Child's Dreams
Growing Up with Spiritual Wisdom—A Guide for Parents and Children

Sri Chinmoy offers practical advice on a subject that is not only an idealist's dream but every concerned parent's lifeline: fostering your child's spiritual life, watching him or her grow up with a love of God and a heart of self-giving.

Topics include: Ensuring your child's spiritual growth • Education and spirituality—their meeting ground • Answers to children's questions about God • A simple guide to meditation and a special section of children's stories guaranteed to delight and inspire. $7.95

The Master and the Disciple

What is a Guru? There are running gurus, diet gurus and even stock market gurus. But to those in search of spiritual enlightenment, the Guru is not merely an 'expert'; he is the way to their self-realisation. Sri Chinmoy says in this definitive book on the Guru-disciple relationship: "The most important thing a Guru does for his spiritual children is to make them aware of something vast and infinite within themselves, which is nothing other than God Himself."

Topics include: How to find a Guru • Telling a real spiritual Master from a false one • How to recognise your own Guru • Making the most spiritual progress while under the guidance of a spiritual Master • What it means when a Guru takes on your *karma* • Plus a special section of stories and plays illustrating the more subtle aspects of the subject. $7.95

Everest-Aspiration

These inspired talks by one who has reached the pinnacle are the best and surest guideposts for others who also want to go upward to the highest, forward to the farthest and inward to the deepest.

Topics include: Dream and Reality • Satisfaction • Imagination • Intuition • Realisation
$8.95

Siddhartha Becomes the Buddha

Who exactly was the Buddha? In these ten dramatic scenes, Sri Chinmoy answers this question from the deepest spiritual point of view. The combination of profound insight and simplicity of language makes this book an excellent choice for anyone, young or old, seeking to understand one of the world's most influential spiritual figures.
$5.95

Peace-Blossom-Fragrance
Aphorisms on Peace

These 700 aphorisms offer a profound and illumining look at the divine nature of peace, it's relation to humanity's age-old quest, and secrets of its attainment and preservation. Special edition not available in stores. $7.95

Flute Music for Meditation

While in a state of deep meditation Sri Chinmoy plays his haunting melodies on the electric echo-flute. Its rich and soothing tones will transport you to the highest realms of inner peace and harmony. (Cassette) $9.95

Inner and Outer Peace

A tapestry of music, poetry and aphorisms on inner and outer peace. Sri Chinmoy's profoundly inspiring messages are woven into a calm and uplifting musical composition with the Master singing, chanting and playing the flute, harmonium, esraj, cello, harpsichord and synthesizer. (Cassette) $9.95

Ecstasy's Trance:
Esraj Music for Meditation

The esraj, often described as a soothing combination of sitar and violin, is Sri Chinmoy's favourite instrument. With haunting intensity, he seems to draw the music from another dimension. The source of these compositions is the silent realm of the deepest and most sublime meditation. Listen to the music and enter this realm, a threshold rarely crossed in the course of one's lifetime. (Cassette) $9.95

The Dance of Light:
Sri Chinmoy Plays the Flute

Forty-seven soft and gentle flute melodies that will carry you directly to the source of joy and beauty: your own aspiring heart. Be prepared to float deep, deep within on waves of music that "come from Heaven itself."   (Cassette) $9.95

To order books or tapes, request a catalogue, or find out more about Sri Chinmoy or the Sri Chinmoy Centres worldwide, please write to:

Aum Publications
86-24 Parsons Blvd.
Jamaica, NY 11432

When ordering a book or cassette, send check or money order made out to Aum Publications. Please add $3.50 postage for the first item and 50¢ for each additional item. Prices valid thru January 1998.